Production Management for Television

Production Management for Television provides an authoritative working guide to this complex and increasingly important task. It is written for those who wish to learn (or learn more) about the detailed and exacting process of managing the creation of television programmes. It is an invaluable resource for students and student productions, as well as those at an early stage in a professional media career or wanting to set up their own production company.

Production Management for Television provides a reliable, factual and theoretical framework for an understanding of production management. It covers:

- the main responsibilities of the Production Manager
- key skills needed by the Production Manager
- routine procedures
- appropriate paperwork and record keeping
- budgeting and scheduling
- Health and Safety issues
- rights management
- career structure and development for Production Managers
- useful references and further information

It is supported by a companion website at www.routledge.com/textbooks/ 9780415424813 where all the forms and spreadsheets discussed can be downloaded.

Leslie Mitchell is Senior Teaching Fellow in the Department of Film, Media and Journalism at Stirling University. He has spent most of his career in various kinds of broadcasting from local and network radio, to regional and network television. He has worked on staff, as a freelance and as an independent producer. He is the author of *Freelancing for Television and Radio* (2005).

Media Skills

SERIES EDITOR: RICHARD KEEBLE, LINCOLN UNIVERSITY
SERIES ADVISERS: WYNFORD HICKS AND JENNY MCKAY

The *Media Skills* series provides a concise and thorough introduction to a rapidly changing media landscape. Each book is written by media and journalism lecturers or experienced professionals and is a key resource for a particular industry. Offering helpful advice and information and using practical examples from print, broadcast and digital media, as well as discussing ethical and regulatory issues, *Media Skills* books are essential guides for students and media professionals.

English for Journalists
3rd edition
Wynford Hicks

Writing for Journalists
2nd edition
Wynford Hicks with Sally Adams, Harriett Gilbert and Tim Holmes

Interviewing for Radio
Jim Beaman

Ethics for Journalists
2nd edition
Richard Keeble

Interviewing for Journalists
2nd edition
Sally Adams, with Wynford Hicks

Researching for Television and Radio
Adèle Emm

Reporting for Journalists
Chris Frost

Subediting for Journalists
Wynford Hicks and Tim Holmes

Designing for Newspapers and Magazines
Chris Frost

Writing for Broadcast Journalists
Rick Thompson

Freelancing for Television and Radio
Leslie Mitchell

Programme Making for Radio
Jim Beaman

Magazine Production
Jason Whittaker

Production Management for Television
Leslie Mitchell

Feature Writing for Journalists
Sharon Wheeler

Production Management for Television

Leslie Mitchell

Routledge
Taylor & Francis Group

LONDON AND NEW YORK

First published 2009
by Routledge
2 Park Square, Milton Park, Abingdon, Oxon OX14 4RN

Simultaneously published in the USA and Canada
by Routledge
711 Third Ave, New York, NY 10017

Routledge is an imprint of the Taylor & Francis Group, an informa business

© 2009 Leslie Mitchell

Typeset in Goudy and Scala Sans by
Florence Production Ltd, Stoodleigh, Devon

British Library Cataloguing in Publication Data
A catalogue record for this book is available from the British Library

Library of Congress Cataloging in Publication Data
Mitchell, Leslie, 1945–.
    Production management for television / Leslie Mitchell.
        p. cm.
    Includes bibliographical references and index.
    1. Television—Production and direction. I. Title.
    PN1992.75.M58 2009
    791.4502'32—dc22   2008039575

ISBN 10: 0–415–42465–8 (hbk)
ISBN 10: 0–415–42481–X (pbk)
ISBN 10: 0–203–88091–9 (ebk)

ISBN 13: 978–0–415–42465–3 (hbk)
ISBN 13: 978–0–415–42481–3 (pbk)
ISBN 13: 978–0–203–88091–3 (ebk)

Contents

Illustrations

Figures

Introduction

I have written this book with two sets of readers in mind. First, there are those who are either at university or are engaged in the study of production and practice in visual media for a variety of platforms, perhaps principally for broadcast television. The second group consists of those already in the industry, possibly working in smaller companies or institutions which do not employ Production Managers as such, yet where the work of production management is vitally important.

It is no accident that this book is entitled *Production Management for Television* rather than *Production Managers for Television* – the emphasis will remain clearly on the tasks; the work which requires to be done in the course of any television production if the production is to be concluded efficiently, safely, on-budget and observing relevant laws and contractual obligations. In many situations, these responsibilities will be carried out by someone called a Production Manager, while equally there are many situations where the work of production management will be done by others with an entirely different job title.

That said, it is also the intention of this book to underline the importance of the role of Production Manager, one which is largely ignored by many of us who teach the practical elements of programme production. I cannot remember a single instance where I have suggested to a student or a recent graduate that they might do well to consider a career as a Production Manager. By contrast, many such discussions have taken place where the centre of attention has been on the other skills required in modern media production; there is no lack of enthusiasm when contemplating a career as a director, producer, sound recordist or editor, yet production management rarely rates a mention. If this book raises the profile of production management and Production Managers then it will have been worthwhile. It will have been even more valuable if it gives encouragement to someone to consider production management as a worthwhile career option when they might not otherwise have thought of it.

I have tried to make this book as practically helpful as possible. It seemed to me to be important to give an account of production management in the real world, as it is practised, even though this may mean a certain blurring of lines between different jobs and varying job descriptions. In terms of what is relevant to Production Managers and the work of production management in general, this book is about good production practice, not about splitting hairs over boundaries.

At times, the terms *employer* and *employment* are used. It should be understood that these are not intended to be strictly legal definitions, but merely used to denote those to whom the Production Manager (or person carrying out a production management task) is responsible in his or her work on a particular production. While on the subject of legal definitions, I would also like to make it clear that this book makes no claim to legal expertise in terms of the rights and responsibilities of producers or production management. I have tried at all points to emphasise that in serious matters such as copyright, licences and Health and Safety, where there are any doubts whatever as to the correct course to take, expert advice (and if necessary legal advice) should be sought. I state this not simply to safeguard myself but because it is sound advice; professional advice taken at the right time can save a great deal of time, anxiety and money later on!

In preparing and writing this book I have sought the help and advice of many Production Managers, as well as those who carry out the work of Production Managers, even though they may not be called PMs. I would like to put on record my gratitude for advice and information so freely given. What I have made of it, of course, is my responsibility and mine alone.

Throughout this book, chapters begin with a quick guide to key concepts covered and wherever it is relevant, boxes present brief summaries of the most important information. You will also find that many forms are presented, and to make life easier for the novice in the world of production management, simple versions of these forms are available online to get you started. The forms are not intended to cover every eventuality, but are offered as a starting point. Their chief virtue I suspect is that they can all be changed, developed and adapted according to the requirements of the individual or production team using them. In this context special thanks are due to my friend and colleague Gordon Ross for a great deal of help with spreadsheets.

Finally, a word about some of the conventions I have adopted in writing the book. Because I know that many members of small production groups will, willingly or not, carry out many of the tasks outlined in this book and yet still never be called Production Managers (because their principal role may be that of producer, director or other job) I have tried to avoid restricting myself to calling them Production Managers, but to refer to them as carrying out the tasks of production management. Accordingly, when I write of those who are so designated, I refer to Production Managers (capitalised). In other circumstances I refer to production management (uncapitalised) to include the whole range of tasks as well as those who carry them out.

Unattributed quotations in the text which follows are exclusively derived from conversations and interviews with those engaged in the task of production management and whose confidentiality I have sought to respect. Occasionally I have clarified the meaning or context of such remarks. These clarifications are mine and are always denoted by [square] brackets.

After a career spent largely in the production of radio and television programmes, as well as in managing a production company, I have thoroughly enjoyed a decade or more of teaching. I owe a debt of gratitude to my colleagues who have taught me much – and to generations of students who have probably taught me as much if not more!

Part I
Production managers

There is no normal day!

... there's a lot of ignorance – when they're looking for work experience, folk always look to producing or directing, never to production management. The pivotal role of the Production Manager is not understood.

1

What is production management?

Quick start definition

Production management: the diligent oversight and direction of all the processes and procedures which are required in order to safely and legally accomplish a finished programme on time and on budget

While the above definition might be a reasonably neat and fairly comprehensive summary, its brevity is in danger of seriously under-estimating the breadth, importance and seriousness of the work it involves. Discussions about the comparative importance of various roles on the production team are largely fatuous, each member and every skill having a unique part to play in the completion of a project. Despite (or possibly because of) this acknowledgement of the collective effort and teamwork required in television production, I make no excuse for emphasising the singular nature of the role of production management, if only because of the largely unregarded, and it has to be said, undervalued, work it represents. It is this crucial contribution that production management makes to the ultimate success (or failure) of the project that should lead us to acknowledge that the accomplishment of the set of tasks it represents is one of the most important in the production process.

Because television production requires creativity and artistry, it is understandable why the so-called *creative* roles receive such attention and are accorded such deference. The director must be allowed to compose the best shots he or she can achieve; in a drama the relationship between cast and director is at the very heart of the creative process. In similar ways it is easy to see how the work of the sound recordist, and later on the editor, are vital. The producer has, among many other responsibilities, the significant task of assembling the talent and the crew. In so many ways it is easy to see how each of these skills makes a vital contribution to every programme. Production management may seem to be a much greyer area. If, however, we return to our original definition and begin to examine it in greater detail we may be surprised at just how important production management is in achieving programme aims and how far-reaching the consequences of failure in this area might be.

Oversight

With the possible exception of the producer, the Production Manager has a unique overview of the programme or series of programmes. This oversight includes a clear appreciation of the creative work of the whole team, but carries with it the added responsibilities brought by an awareness of the parameters of time and budget, and all the other constraints of programme production.

Diligence

Thomas Edison's often repeated definition of genius that it is 'one per cent inspiration and ninety-nine per cent perspiration' is an apt description of the diligence that is required of those engaged in production management. Edison's saying might have become clichéd by repetition, but it is so often repeated because like most clichés it contains an important grain of truth. Much of the work of the Production Manager is detailed and painstaking and requires great accuracy. Paperwork which might seem boring and irritating to some will be seen in proper perspective by the Production Manager; thus risk assessments, properly carried out and duly recorded and filed may well prevent accidents and will certainly assist in the investigation of any incidents which do occur. Edison provides us with a welcome reminder that discipline, organisation and attention to detail may well be essential to provide a framework within which creativity can thrive – which come to think of it, is not a bad alternative description of the work of the Production Manager!

Processes

An understanding of the processes by which television programmes come to be made is an essential part of the stock-in-trade of production management. Without this *inside knowledge* a Production Manager will be ill-equipped to make decisions quickly and wisely. Should, for instance, a director be allowed an extra day's shooting, despite the strains that this might place on the budget? The answer to this question will, of course, depend on the circumstances – which is precisely the point. A well-informed understanding of the difficulties of this particular shoot is essential. The location, the cast, the vagaries of the weather and indeed the history and track-record of the particular director in keeping to the agreed shooting schedule are simply some of the myriad factors to be taken into account by the Production Manager when making the decision. Such a decision may be required quickly, the result of an anxious telephone conversation from a distant location. It is clearly important that in such circumstances the decision is soundly based. In summary, a knowledge of industry processes provides those involved in production management with the ability to understand and therefore to be sympathetic to the requirements of each member of the team. The answer may not always be to the liking of the individual making the request but usually it will be respected if it is treated with the sympathy which comes from an understanding of the skills, needs and contributions of every team member.

Procedures

An appreciation of the processes by which programmes are made is complemented by an intimate knowledge of the procedures required to complete these processes successfully. By this I mean the tasks (often defined by completing a form or producing a report) which are required by others. At times these others will be colleagues in the same company or organisation. For example, monthly financial reports may be required by the head of finance in an independent production company. If such reports are not completed and submitted on time, then the financial stability of the company itself and the ability to forecast cash flow might be jeopardised, let alone the consequences to the programme in production. An example of a procedure that is required by an organisation external to the company might be that of music logging and reporting. While the completion of the actual task may well not be the responsibility of the Production Manager, making sure that it is done and that logs are sent to the appropriate body certainly is.

Safely

Television crews inhabit a dangerous world; the risks they face on a daily basis are generally far greater than those encountered by the general public. And I am not thinking here of foreign shoots in dangerous war zones or the obvious risks to life and limb when you *doorstep* a shoddy or fraudulent craftsman at his own home! Production teams need to be constantly reminded of the risks of using their own equipment on location or in a studio for that matter. Cables, heavy objects, camera rigs (and sometimes other members of the crew simply doing their job) pose threats to personal safety. It usually falls to the Production Manager to provide these reminders to each team and to ensure that each member has received the appropriate Health and Safety training, so that the risks can be evaluated and minimised. Chapter 6 goes on to deal with this important subject in greater detail.

Legally

The public nature of television production, whether or not it results in a broadcast, involves publication of some sort – as a corporate video, a podcast or a DVD, for example. So in addition to the legal framework to which every individual and corporate body is subject, there are areas of regulation which are specific to the media and are contained in legislation such as the various Broadcasting Acts (for example, Broadcasting Act 1990, 1996, Communications Act, 2003) and other measures. It is clearly not the responsibility of the Production Manager to be an expert in the law, but an awareness of the areas which are subject to rules and regulation is essential – even if only to remain alert to issues where professional advice is essential. There are many legal issues from child protection to decency, product placement, copyright and many others. Again these areas, generally grouped under the heading of *compliance*, will be discussed in greater detail in later chapters; it is enough for now to make the point that production management requires a good pair of legal antennae to anticipate potential problems and to avoid disasters!

On time

Time management is probably one of the greatest responsibilities within production management. Another cliché claims that *time is money*; it is a cliché that is certainly true for television. Time seems to be of the essence of everything to do with production, from the weeks budgeted for every member of a crew, the days the presenter is booked for, the hours in the edit suite, and of course the *running time* in minutes and seconds of the final production. Everything is timed to the hour, minute or second and ensuring the observance of the agreed timing is often the role of the Production Manager.

On budget

The programme budget may 'belong' to the producer; it will no doubt have been negotiated by the producer or the executive producer, but responsibility for remaining within budget, for ensuring that the limits of individual cost centres are observed and that reports are accurately compiled and maintained, remains with production management. It is a huge responsibility; often, as we shall see, it means saying 'no' even when you would rather say 'yes'. The cost of television production continues to rise, while at the same time budgets are pared back; so there is real pressure to make every penny count, and in the day-to-day life of the production office, this pressure falls largely on the Production Manager.

In summary

This brief analysis of the definition at the beginning of this chapter, demonstrates if nothing else that production management is a central, vital and rather undervalued part of the process of making television programmes.

In the sections and chapters which follow we will be looking at production management in three distinct but interrelated ways. By doing so, I hope that the needs of the reader will be met in the most helpful manner. So in the next chapter, *Production management as a career*, we will be thinking of production management as a distinct and defined role within a company or organisation, in other words we will be looking at the job of being a Production Manager and benefiting from the experience of some of those who have been doing it for quite a while. At the same time we need to recognise that the work of production management may well be done by a member of the production team who is not officially designated as a Production Manager. Indeed the work may be divided in a formal or informal way between different members of a production unit. The recognition of the fact that the work of production management might well be spread over a number of different members of a production team means that Part II of this book is focused on skills and techniques rather than on a particular individual called a Production Manager. Many, if not most, student productions do not have a designated Production Manager (I often wonder if the resulting productions might have been better had they done so!). I have had close contact with BBC productions where various management tasks are shared by all members of the team with a relatively light-touch administrative coordinating role undertaken by a producer, senior producer or executive producer. The precise detail of the organisation of how this is to be achieved is less important than the crucial point that the tasks need to be completed as and when required in as transparent a manner as possible and to the satisfaction of the relevant company or commissioner.

Production management – the personal perspective

In order to gain an insight into their daily lives, I asked a number of those engaged in production management if they could describe a typical working day. This is an almost impossible question to answer especially when, as we shall see, the work varies so enormously from day to day. Their answers do, however, provide a colourful, subjective and valuable glimpse of what life can be like when you are a Production Manager.

> There is no normal day!
>
> If I am working on a documentary or a magazine [programme], I am at the computer most of the day.
>
> On a big budget production I keep the figures up to date every day. On *Big Brother* I might be off buying their posh meal; literally carrying food into the Big Brother House . . . being responsible for noise limits [re: neighbours] in the BB house, liaising with the local council about late night filming with lights.

No day is ever the same, depending on the production cycle and the genre. You wake up wondering what's likely to go wrong today! It can feel like you're constantly treading on egg shells. You may feel it is all under control . . . then bang! A crisis comes along and takes your time and energy. [You might get] . . . a call from an edit suite – the tapes have been [accidentally] left back in the office. A problem that takes a minute to arise can take an hour at least to solve. So there is no typical day, you just have to respond to what's happening, it is about multitasking and understanding the basic principles of TV.

[I may have a] meeting about schedules, plans for filming – [working out] how much time in filming days, fees for location.

Maybe phone calls from another team in 'post' [production] in the London office – an example might be issues over credits, (we would have to liaise with Broadcaster when the credits need to be on four cards [screens] and not on the agreed three.

There could be phone calls because of a personality clash between a freelance editor and company production staff . . .

. . . meanwhile I am liaising with a commissioning editor about co-production, about the proportion of money to be put up by each party because there's production company-broadcaster and a charity organisation involved.

. . . and what I was actually trying to do was my cost reports for the financial controller.

Despite the obviously stressful situations described in these fragmentary conversations (or possibly because of them) every Production Manager I spoke to, without exception, thoroughly enjoyed the work they did and appeared to thrive on the trouble-shooting and enabling role they so clearly occupied.

2
Production management as a career

One of the big problems in the sector is that too many young people who are coming into the industry know nothing about the coordination role – and remember 'coordination' is the crucial word.

Quick start definitions

Indie: Industry shorthand for Independent Production Company, as distinct from a Broadcasting organisation such as the BBC or ITV

Production Coordinator: A responsible but junior production management role often involved in booking equipment and facilities, book-keeping, etc. A possible career step before becoming a Production Manager

P.M.: Industry shorthand for the Production Manager

P.A.: In the media industries usually production assistant, though it can refer to the more generic 'personal assistant'

O.B.: Outside Broadcast

The responsibilities outlined in the preceding chapter may seem somewhat daunting. The accurate completion of the tasks involved can have an enormous impact on the success of a programme or series and indeed on the viability and financial health of the company, especially if it is a small one. In such circumstances the inevitable question arises as to why anyone would volunteer for the job, let alone actively seek it! I have to say at this point that in meeting a number of Production Managers, in connection with this book, I was enormously struck by the enthusiasm that so many of them expressed. Clearly they love their work and its challenges, yet they harbour no illusions when they describe the challenges, pitfalls and downsides of the job.

It might be thought logical to start this chapter by considering the routes into the work of the Production Manager, the career structure and the training that is available before and during a career in this field. However, I have been particularly impressed by the personal qualities of the Production Managers I have met and by the importance that these qualities might well have not only in the enjoyment of the work but in the ability to do the job and to cope with the inevitable pressures it brings. This chapter, at least in the earlier stages, relies very heavily on the conversations I have enjoyed with a number of Production Managers and on their ideas and assessments of what the job involves and the qualities it demands of those undertaking it. There are, of course, no hard and fast rules – I have been impressed not only by the degree of unanimity expressed by those I have met but also by the variety and differences in approach that they have outlined. The scope and responsibility of the Production Manager remains largely constant throughout a major broadcaster like the BBC. Here the significant variations occur in different genres. The most obvious division is that between drama and the other areas of output, though there are also different ways of working in studio-based and live outside broadcast (OB) programming.

Essentially the role of Production Manager is the same whatever the genre, though the tools and methods used to achieve goals may be quite different. A later chapter explores the peculiarities of script break-down which are commonplace to the Production Manager working in drama features, but unfamiliar territory to someone working in factual programming.

While these genre differences are also to be found in independent production companies, (indies), in this sector there is a greater variation in the approach to defining the role of the Production Manager and this seems largely to be a function of the particular way in which the individual company has evolved and organised itself and its productions. It is therefore important that anyone seeking employment with a particular company or broadcaster should familiarise themselves with the detail of how that potential employer defines the duties and responsibilities of the Production Manager. To give a brief and fairly obvious example, while tracking budgets is a significant part of any Production Manager's job, in some companies this will take up the majority of the PM's time. Clearly this might not appeal to some individuals who would prefer the variety offered by the role within a different and more varied environment. Similarly, some organisations will require a Production Manager to work simultaneously across a variety of production teams, while others (perhaps more commonly) will have a dedicated PM for each production. Again such variations will have a significant impact on the job satisfaction (or otherwise) of the individual.

It is easy to define the role of a camera operator or director, for example; their tasks are relatively unchanging as they move from one programme to the next. It is, however, much less easy to define a universal template for the work of Production Manager, especially outside the realm of the major broadcaster or a very large independent production company. It is in the interests of anyone seeking employment in this area to enquire how a potential employer defines the work and its responsibilities. Despite such variations, every Production Manager will be quick to point out that adaptability and the ability to cope quickly and competently with a rapidly changing set of circumstances are part of the essential armoury of the job.

The question 'is this the right career for me?' is one which demands an answer. As we discover how the industry and those working in it define production management and the qualities required to undertake it successfully, the answer should become clearer. The Production Managers I have spoken to have a very high level of job satisfaction – if you are seriously contemplating a career in this field, you should not overlook the importance of this as a consideration. Competence in your work is important; enjoying it (at least most of the time) is more important and will ultimately ensure your continuing competence.

Personal qualities – the industry perspective

I asked a number of Production Managers to think about the personal qualities they thought were important to anyone undertaking this work. Here in direct quotations are some of their answers; the headings are mine:

Approachable

You need to be approachable and calm, to be able to see the bigger picture. If changes are needed then you can't freak but need to find a positive way forward. You can't be a scary person to the team. If [you have a crew] filming abroad and you get a 3 a.m. call that a radio mic has broken, or they just call for a moan – you can't say 'I can't talk to you at the moment' especially if they're in Afghanistan!

Organised

To be organised, organisational skills, you need to be calm under pressure. If everything goes wrong, it is you who gets it – if someone doesn't turn up on a shoot – it is down to you. If there's not enough time for an edit . . .

Organised! I am famous for my lists. Every morning I come in, make my list of things to do, retype my list in a Word document separated into projects. I am a list person. I use Outlook for reminders. [So I may] realise someone will be on holiday, and there's a task to be done.

Patient

You must have a lot of patience, some team members need their hands held through everything!

Level-headed

. . . if you get stressed or are a flapper, you would probably end up being committed! Also you need to be able to cope with long hours. You're in early to make sure everything's ready then you're the last to leave because you're getting stuff ready for the following day.

Crises incur costs and mean you have to find money from limited budgets. You need to be transparent and make sure things are not spiralling out of control.

Assertive

> Thorough, assertive, level-headed and cool.
>
> Your personality needs to be able to stand up to the producer, there's always a tension – you feel you are constantly on people's backs. Cock-ups, accidents, minor prangs with vehicles, tapes missing. Many things can go astray.

Clearly to possess such a range of qualities and to exercise them consistently would qualify any individual for sainthood let alone career success and promotion! Nevertheless these reflections offer a valuable insight into personal disciplines which may be refined and developed with experience, as most of the contributors have had the opportunity to do over many years. They certainly should not discourage those who are perhaps less confident of their own resilience.

Becoming a Production Manager

Despite the fact that we may like to think otherwise, career decisions are often less to do with rational and determined decisions and pathways and more to do with the opportunities which present themselves at particular moments. This is certainly the case with many of the Production Managers I have spoken to, most of whom have 'fallen into' the work as a result of individual circumstances rather than as a result of a clearly planned career path.

The secretarial route

A number of Production Managers started their media careers by working in some kind of secretarial role, either as a production secretary, or possibly by working as a personal assistant to a senior television executive. In such cases, experience has been obtained by working in a production environment. In some cases the fact that an individual has been working with a senior executive (even if in a relatively junior role) has meant that they have been exposed to policy decisions, meetings with other senior executives, and most importantly the commissioning editors of client broadcasters. The experience gained in such an environment is clearly very helpful in a future as a Production Manager; knowledge is gained in many areas of the media business both inside the company and with external organisations and individuals:

> I started as a PA (Personal Assistant) to the Managing Director [of a very large independent production company], this gave me the opportunity to get to know commissioning departments. Then as a Production Assistant, I learned production 'on the job'. One of the big problems in the sector is that too many young people who are coming into the industry know nothing about the coordination role – and remember 'coordination' is the crucial word.

> I came into this work via the secretarial route. I did an English degree then I joined a small indie as a Production Secretary. After that I worked on location as a Production Assistant then as a Researcher.

The production route

This is probably the most common pathway to production management; experience of the production process is essential and some of those in a number of production roles discover that they have both an aptitude and an appetite for organisation and coordination. Sometimes the process of change will be subtle and almost unnoticed as the individual finds that they are taking on more responsibility for the management of the production. Indeed we should remind ourselves that in many cases, production management roles are taken on by members of the team; producers, directors and production assistants for example, who are not specifically designated as Production Managers:

> [My company] has always given the production management role to producers, then they appointed one Production Manager as such. Originally I was offered the job of producer; then I made a gradual move into production management, and encouraged by my Managing Director, my work spread across many productions.

> I worked in programme finance [for a broadcaster] so I dealt with indies and contracts and so I had a good point of view,

this brings an understanding of how the sector works . . . things like Union agreements . . .

After University I got a job as a BBC researcher then became an Assistant Producer before I worked as a Production Manager, so I definitely came through a production route.

Most people [coming into the job] have a media degree. But there's a lot of ignorance – when they're looking for work experience folk always look to producing or directing, never to production management. The pivotal role of the Production Manager is not understood.

Education and qualifications

Clearly production management is not 'entry level' work. A detailed and comprehensive understanding of production issues is essential to do this job and such insights take time to acquire.

It is very difficult to make broad generalisations about the educational qualifications you need to work in production management. In television generally, education is probably more important than qualification. What I mean is that an ability to think clearly, to look for information and to know where to look for it, along with a good range of interpersonal skills, are really going to count in the business. When the BBC recruits for its training schemes it has this to say:

> Trainees are recruited according to their talent, potential and passion to achieve great things with us, rather than their formal academic backgrounds.

This is not suggesting that academic education is not important but it does suggest that the fact that you *have* studied is possibly more important than *what* you have studied. A university degree or college certificate or diploma shows that you have the ability, self-discipline and motivation to follow a course and see it through to the end. Nevertheless there are many people in television who have no formal qualifications at a higher level and who do very well. However, they may well have had to spend a disproportionate amount of time developing particular skills and experience to compensate for the lack of formal training. Unless you have a very strong conviction that you wish to enter an occupation within broadcasting that does require particular qualifications, it is probably wise to study something that really engages and interests you; in such circumstances you are more likely to learn more and profit from your education. In its turn this will mean that you have more to offer to a potential employer.

Do I need a media studies degree?

One of the questions most frequently asked by young people who have ambitions to work in television is 'Do I need a media studies degree?' The answer to that particular question is simple and it is 'No – you do not need a media studies degree.' The question is so simply answered because it is the wrong question. 'How helpful is a media studies degree in finding employment?' is a far more interesting question and the answers are more interesting to you if you are seriously contemplating work in the media either as a permanent employee or as a freelance.

Skillset (the Sector Skills Council for Creative Media) figures derived from their 2005 workforce survey indicate that 69 per cent were graduates, 30 per cent had a degree in media studies and 28 per cent had a post-graduate degree. (Skillset Survey of Audio Visual Industries' Workforce 2005 [Internet] Available: www.skillset.org/uploads/pdf/asset_7964.pdf [accessed 23 August 2008].)

There are some clear advantages that a degree in media studies will bestow, including:

- An understanding of the nature and structure of the media industries
- A knowledge of the ownership and control of the media
- A study of the impact and influences of the media on society
- A study of media texts and structures.

In addition, depending on the course of study, more practical production elements may give an insight into:

- Editorial decision-making
- Pitching and programme proposals
- Health and Safety
- Audiovisual recording techniques
- Editing.

It is hard to see how an education which includes some or all of these elements could fail to provide a good starting point for work in the audiovisual industry. However, we need to bear in mind that because production management is not an entry level job, what is likely to be of far more importance is the experience and training obtained *on the job*, after graduation.

What kind of degree is most helpful in production management?

It is clear that a very large proportion of graduates working in the audiovisual industry have media-related qualifications, and that there are more media graduates than graduates of all other subjects put together. That this should be so is hardly surprising and somewhat gives the lie to those who constantly detract from the value of media studies as a proper subject of academic study.

The main advantages of a degree of any kind consist in the benefits that academic study brings; the ability to reason logically, to pursue enquiry and to be guided by fact and not assumption or prejudice. In addition, the ability to express and present oneself in writing as well as in person and a degree of confidence in doing so are important outcomes of a good course. It can be argued that the precise course of study is ultimately of less importance, though of course this depends very much on your intended employment. It is difficult to give clear or precise advice on the undergraduate courses which might be useful for a future career in production management. A degree in politics or international relations may be of enormous value to you if you want to work in the production of current affairs, news or documentaries; equally business studies or accountancy might be just as valuable in your budgeting role! Those who intend to be engaged in production management of drama will find a degree in English, drama or performing arts particularly relevant. In these circumstances such a degree may well be of far more value than a media studies degree.

Is there a career structure for Production Managers?

Just as there is no formal route into production management, neither is there a specifically definable career path, although the experience of many

Production Managers suggests that it is possible to discern some common pathways in developing a career is this field. At the less experienced level, production management work may begin as an assistant producer or researcher. Production Coordinators (as the name suggests) undertake a number of roles associated with production management, usually under the supervision of a PM or Unit Manager or Senior Producer. Such work may involve much of the day-to-day organisation and distribution of schedules, travel booking, location catering and other practical issues. Again it should be remembered that every company will have its own way of organising these matters and of distributing the responsibilities of production management, so that only the most general outline can be given here. However, it is quite clear that the role of Production Coordinator is a key steppingstone to the greater responsibility of Production Manager. Production Managers may ultimately find promotion and increased responsibility in a variety of roles, as Unit Managers, for example, taking responsibility for strands of programming or output genres. A variation of this career path may well involve an increasing role within the business and planning roles of companies and organisations at a senior managerial level. The Head of Production of one major indie gained a great deal of the experience and expertise to undertake that senior role while working as a Production Manager. As in many employment sectors, such a career may well benefit from continuing training and education, and a number of courses, both short and long, are increasingly available to those who already have some experience and background in production.

Career development and training

The major organisations providing practical training for production management are the NFTS (National Film and Television School) (www.nftsfilm-tv.ac.uk/) and indies' trade association, PACT (Producers' Alliance for Cinema and Television). Understandably, provision of such courses and their precise content will vary as demand for them changes. Full details of these organisations and others providing training in production management can be found in the directory in Part IV of this book. At the time of writing, for example, the NFTS offers a 12-month course in production management for those who already have some experience in the film or television industry. Interestingly (and encouragingly), the NFTS introduction to the course asserts that:

There are few jobs that are changing faster than that of the Production Manager. From data management to delivering programmes on multiple platforms, the role of the Production Manager has expanded so widely that many PMs are now full partners in running companies, rather than being sidelined in middle management.

PACT's training is now undertaken by the Indie Training Fund (www.indietrainingfund.com) and courses are only open to employees of companies which are members of the fund. Direct provision is made for production management training as such and courses are also provided in core areas such as Health and Safety and copyright issues.

Skillset, the Sector Skills Council, will provide an overview of training available to those with varying levels of experience in production management. Skillset supports and subsidises, among others, a short two-day introductory course in production management.

BBC training does not at the time of writing offer overarching training for production management; it does however offer short courses in a number of areas which are fundamental to the work of PMs. These include risk management and, interestingly, personal effectiveness, including assertiveness and communication skills. It may well be advisable for anyone seeking to increase specific skills to look beyond the usual suppliers of training for this sector and to find courses which are related to distinctive skills such as project management, media economics and business skills.

Finally, it is worth pointing the reader in the direction of the many post-graduate courses on offer from various universities and colleges. These may vary from the University of Brighton's postgraduate Masters' degree in Digital Television Management and Production (www.brighton.ac.uk) to my own department's MSc in Media Management at the University of Stirling (www.fmj.stir.ac.uk).

Part II
Skills and techniques

In the following five chapters, we will be looking in some depth at the skills and techniques which underlie the work of production management in a number of key areas. Then in the following third section of the book, we will set about applying these skills and techniques at the relevant stage in the production process.

The idea of Part II is to offer some basic understanding of the qualities and abilities (many of them personal) required to carry out production in a logical, step-by-step process. Some readers may have a mastery of a number of these areas, but hopefully there will be some material with which they are not already familiar and which therefore will be helpful. Others will find themselves on unfamiliar ground from the outset. Perhaps I should make it clear that I write not as an experienced Production Manager, but as one who has spent a few decades dedicated to managing productions, from regular television series with complicated and extremely demanding studio schedules and budgets to one-off corporate productions which can be just as demanding, if not more so. I have, of course, to acknowledge a huge indebtedness to the experience of others, who unlike me have spent a large portion of their careers in professional production management of one kind or another. In other words, much of what I pass on, I have learned from others. These words are not intended as mere lip service or ingratiation but seek to recognise that like most others in this industry, the vast majority of the skills I have developed, the techniques I have learned and the abilities I have gained, have been passed on by others, freely and generously. As a young and inexperienced producer/director working for the BBC, often on *live* outside broadcasts, the best tip I was ever given was to listen carefully to the skilled people working alongside me. As that young and inexperienced person I often found myself responsible for large crews of camera operators, sound, vision control, engineers and floor managers. Although, as the producer and often director too, I was technically *in charge* of the whole outfit, my leadership had to be tempered and informed by a recognition of the fact that not only did I need the experience and skill of those around me, but that their contribution could add immeasurably to the quality of the resulting programme. Balancing assertiveness with an ability to take advice and help is a key personal skill and pretty essential in any kind of management, production or otherwise, television or not. If those around you do not offer advice or assistance, ask yourself if you are listening enough or carefully enough. If members of a crew or a production team do offer such help, to accept is not a sign of weakness but a recognition on your part of the skills and experience your team has to offer. Remember that human beings offer help to those they trust and respect. The converse is also true!

After a general discussion of each skill or technique, which needs to be developed and used by the Production Manager, we will consider a number of key approaches and practical recommendations.

3
Managing time

A recent quick and crude search of a large Internet bookstore on the subject 'Time Management' instantly revealed a staggering ten thousand suggestions for further reading. Most of the titles promise that they will reveal the real secrets of how to get through work efficiently, quickly and painlessly in order to leave more time free for personal enjoyment and refreshment. If only it were so easy! However, we should not be too quick to dismiss such advice. First, the proliferation of titles on the subject suggests that it sells well. This in turn suggests that many of us feel that we could improve the way we manage our time, and therefore our work. We all have a fixed and limited time at our disposal; no matter how hard we try we cannot manufacture more of it, that is why it is such a precious commodity. So time management is really about making the best possible use of the time that is available to us, and not wasting it. If you have no problem organising your time and completing given tasks according to an agreed deadline, then maybe you do not need this chapter, or at least a quick skim will suffice. There is, however, a further question that perhaps we need to ask ourselves when considering the subject of time management. This question is about stress. On a personal note, I can confess that although I am relatively efficient, and do not generally miss deadlines or appointments or omit to do important things, this is often at the cost of a great deal of stress. I may wake up in the night and worry about a task I have not started or am in danger of omitting or forgetting. I may worry, and often do, that I will not be able to complete everything I have to do in the time that is available to me. Consequently I sometimes feel that I could have completed a task more efficiently, thoroughly and enjoyably than I actually did. Stress can be a positive driving force, providing us with just the right amount of personal adrenalin to energise us into completing tasks. On the other hand, stress can also be tiring and demoralising, robbing us of the enjoyment and satisfaction we might otherwise derive from completing the jobs for which we are responsible.

This chapter is therefore based on the assumption that you feel that it is possible to improve not only the efficiency with which you carry out the management of production tasks, but that you would also like to keep the stress involved at a reasonable level. I am, of course, making the assumption that you are principally concerned with the good management of your own time – if you can do that, you will be in a much better position to manage time for other people on your production team.

For reasons which should now be fairly obvious, I have read a few books on time management. It is fair to say that each one really has had something to offer. None of it, of course, is rocket science; most of it is fairly basic common sense, but none the worse for that. The benefit of such books is that at their best they encourage us to focus on improving our performance and to think about how we organise our lives. The drawback is that in offering their own particular 'system' they can become prescriptive and rigid and not adaptable to life as we experience it. Even worse, such systems may induce feelings of guilt if we do not match the high standards they advocate; guilt leads to stress and so the danger is that we may end up as less efficient than when we started. So you may find it helpful to read a book about time management. I make one or two suggestions in the reference section of this book; however, a search engine or bookstore will quickly reveal many thousands more. My only guidance as you choose is that you avoid the quackery of miracle cure self-help books! The more modest the claims, the more likely it will be that the book is useful and will give you general principles to help you organise your life and your work. I would strongly suggest that you do not read more than one, or at the most, two books. In this way you will avoid the danger of the 'quest for the holy grail' of time management. Such a quest will be very interesting, you will come across many schemes, you will be offered expensive subscriptions by many a guru. If you enjoy playing at your computer, then you will be able to try out many pieces of software to help you in your search. While you are engaged on this search, you will however be neglecting the tasks you are striving to achieve more efficiently. In other words, you will be wasting the very time you are trying to manage.

You may be considering taking on the work of production management possibly for the first time. You might be working for yourself or for a small company and do not have the 'luxury' of a dedicated post for a Production Manager at this point. Alternatively you may be working on a student production and have been given the responsibility of managing the production (and your wayward, if creative, colleagues). If you wish to become more efficient in the management of your time and of the production you are undertaking, then the following paragraphs are offered as some help to get you on track.

At the risk of setting myself up as a time management guru (which I am emphatically not), I offer some practical and simple advice which should be more than enough for those taking on the responsibilities of production management for the first time.

One of the fundamental objectives of most sensible help offered by the myriad sources available is to get the tasks out of your head and to stop relying on your memory. This is not to imply for a moment that your memory is defective, it might be very good indeed, but your memory is not necessarily equipped to remind you at the right time that a task is due to be completed, nor will your memory naturally prioritise your tasks. So in getting the tasks out of your head you will be better placed to arrange reminders for their completion; you will also be in a position to prioritise them rationally and as you think best. A further advantage of getting things out of your head is that you will reduce the stress which is always induced by having a number of things you need to remember constantly bumping around in your brain!

I suppose that what I am proposing here is that you try to de-clutter your head. While we are at it, we might suggest too that you de-clutter your working area too, and that means your desk. This is not always easy, it is something I always find I have to work hard at. I know to my cost that if my working environment is untidy, I lose things very quickly. The busier I get, the more I tend to clutter my office; the more things I misplace in the clutter, the quicker I become stressed, anxious and inefficient. So a first step on the road to production management efficiency might be to take control and tidy up your work environment, then you can make a start on the mental workplace, your brain!

I am sure that by now you are at least one step ahead. If you are to reduce what is in your head then where are these items to go? The obvious answer is, of course, that they form a list. Every single Production Manager I have spoken to is a self-confessed lists freak. They manage their lists in a variety of ways, but they all have their lists. This all seems so simple as to be obvious and hardly worthy of extended discussion. Nevertheless, it is an area we need to pursue. Again, on a personal note, though I am pretty good at making lists, I am far less good at keeping them by me, consulting them and ticking off the tasks as I achieve them. Consequently I still constantly have to remember things, and we have already discussed the disadvantages of carrying around too much *stuff* in the head. Again, what I have picked up from practising PMs is that they often re-write their lists. This is a good way of adding and deleting items both as new tasks arise and old ones are completed. This then is a list system at its most basic. Yet it is also extremely flexible. If you are starting to use the system, probably writing the list, prioritising and reviewing it might only need to happen each day when you reach your desk or wherever you happen to be working. As you become busier, or your workload becomes more complex, you simply need to increase the frequency with which the list is updated. Some people in production management I know keep separate lists for personal and business purposes, others prefer a combined list – whatever suits you best.

Basic list-making

- *Make your list*
- *Review it*
- *Prioritise it*
- *Re-write it*
- *Review it*

Maybe we already need to add a couple of items to this list already. As I pointed out earlier, it is all very well to excel at making lists, but we have also to train ourselves to consult them quite often. And then one final point in this section. It is great to have instituted such a list system in our lives, but we need to recognise that for it to be successful we still actually need to complete the tasks on the list. No system that fails to recognise the act of will and the necessity of self-discipline will ever help us to manage the limited resource of time. Used effectively and consistently, the list will enable us to leave our brains free to think constructively without relying on memory and panic. It will reduce stress and in time provide its own reinforcement by having the habitual satisfaction of seeing tasks completed on time and with reduced stress. Incidentally, one helpful tip is to include vital information on the list too. It can be incredibly irritating if you have made a note to call someone, but have not included the number to call. It really will help to make sure that you lift the phone at the right time if the number is there, on the list and you do not have to chase round to find it. If you are then clever enough to keep your old lists somewhere safe, you never know when those jotted down pieces of information are going to be a lifesaver.

Basic list making – reviewed!

- *Make your list*
- *Review the list*
- *Prioritise the list*
- *Re-write the list*
- *Consult the list*
- *Do the tasks!*

One incidental benefit of having such a list system habitually in place in our lives is that in production management terms it puts us in a far better position to deal with the unexpected. The trouble with crises, even when we cope with them, is that they tend to drive everything else out of our minds. How often are we tempted to blame our failure to complete an important task on something that came up unexpectedly? If your list is in good shape and up to date, it will be there to go back to and will help you to pick up the pieces when the crisis has been resolved.

It is, of course, possible to use systems which are far more sophisticated than the simple paper-based list. Immensely powerful computer programs such as Microsoft Outlook enable lists of tasks to be combined with all your email information, calendars and contact lists. The advantage of a computer-based system like this is the integration it offers between these various items of information and reminders which can be set as tasks that need to be completed. Lists can, of course, be printed out and with a little investigation and patience can even be printed on forms which match paper-based systems such as Filofax and other proprietary information managers. The obvious disadvantage of such a system is that it is not especially portable and is more suited to those who tend to work consistently from their desk rather than on location. Printouts are all very well but the input of data is not so easily achieved away from the comforting presence of the computer. Rapidly changing technology will no doubt make the computerised personal information manager (PIM) more portable and user-friendly. Blackberry and similar devices have enthusiastic users, and they do offer a very attractive integration of personal organiser, email and phone facilities. They are, however, not cheap to use or operate and probably do not offer the ease of use of the conventional keyboard that most Production Managers would require as they carry out their work. We will return to the whole question of time and management in Chapter 5, when we think about how to create and manage schedules.

Summary points – managing time

- *Take control*
- *De-clutter your desk and working environment*
- *If you need to, read a book on time-management*
- *Do not rely on your memory – however good!*
- *Find a list system that suits you – trust it and stick with it*
- *Commit your tasks to a list*
- *Make your lists as simple as possible*
- *Re-write and prioritise your lists as often as needed*
- *Put basic information like phone numbers into your lists – it saves time later*
- *Put deadlines into your lists*
- *Remember, however good your list is – you still have to carry out the task!*

4
Creating and managing budgets

Introduction

In this chapter, we will look first at some of the basic concepts behind programme budgeting, starting by asking the question 'What is a budget?' We then go on to build a fairly simple budget for a short factual programme using a spreadsheet to make our calculations. At the end of the chapter, we will consider some of the changes we need to make to our outline budget for a factual programme in order to make a suitable template for a simple drama production.

There is absolutely no doubt that managing budgets is one of the most important tasks of production management. Ensuring that the programme comes in 'on budget' is the bottom line of the job. This chapter will provide a step-by-step outline for preparing a fairly simple budget and will then go on to look more closely at the tasks involved in maintaining that budget. Again, none of the work involved, even in building a budget from scratch, is rocket science. Some experience of book-keeping is unquestionably helpful, yet lack of this experience need not deter anyone whose job it is to manage a production. On the other hand, it is not uncommon for experienced Production Managers to seek additional training in accountancy and business management skills in order to enhance the contribution they can make to their employers' businesses and by extension to their own career prospects. At the other end of the spectrum, student productions and small company productions also need budgets to be well planned and maintained. You could argue that it is more crucial to successfully manage small budgets than big ones, for the simple fact is that small budgets are more quickly exhausted and need tighter control. In the world of television all budgets, big or small, have to be closely monitored. There is no quicker way for a company to fail than to neglect programme budgets; programme commissioners will be wary of accepting new ideas and pitches from a producer who has failed to bring in programmes on budget.

Budgets provide much of the creative (and uncreative) tension in production teams. Producers and directors are, quite rightly, narrowly focused on getting the best possible content for the programme and inevitably there will be many occasions when they feel they need that extra day's filming or further items of technical equipment that were not in the original costings. No wonder then that one of the core personal qualities of the PM is that of assertiveness. It takes a strong personality to withstand perfectly proper requests for extensions to the budget, and a fine sense of judgment to balance the competing claims of programme quality and budgetary prudence. In addition, the person in charge of the budget needs to remain on good terms with every member of the team, while at the same time refusing requests for further expenditure, if such a refusal is justified. It does not take a Production Manager long to work out which the members of the team will routinely demand more resources, and those whose requests need to be taken more seriously.

Because such experiences are commonplace in most productions, PMs have evolved strategies for dealing positively with these eventualities. There are four possible outcomes when there is a need to contemplate overspending in one area of the budget:

1   **Refusal**: As I have suggested above, there may well be a perfectly good reason for turning down such a request. It is probably wise not to get involved in a protracted discussion as to whether or not such additional expenditure would enhance the quality of the programme. To engage at this level would mean questioning the creative judgement of a member of the team who is employed to make such judgments. The nub of the argument is whether the extra expenditure and the consequent pressure on the budget is justified or even possible. This is a less sensitive, though no less tricky area for dispute. Your response will depend on your previous experience (if any) of the member of team making the request and will possibly require recourse to the producer or series producer for further advice.

Let us assume for the moment that there is some case to be made for a modest increase in resources in the area requested – it might, for example, be a request for that extra day for shooting or editing:

2   **Juggle the budget!** What is imperative is the maintenance of the overall budget; variations within it are less important than the *bottom line*. As the Production Manager you will be tracking all the budget headings (known also as cost centres). You may well be aware of underspends in some areas. If you can be confident that such underspends will be maintained you might be able to justify overspending, say, on editing costs if you can balance that by an identical underspend on travel and transport.

3   **Use the contingency**: Every budget should have a modest percentage, up to 10 per cent of the total, set aside (possibly secretly) which can be used at the discretion of the person controlling the budget when situations arise which demand that unforeseen costs are met. This is known as contingency. After all, every budget is an estimate even though it needs to be as accurate and future-proof as it possibly can be. The key is to make good use of this experience and to make sure that you take account of what happened to stretch the budget on one programme to prepare you better as you plan the next one. You might, for example, come to realise that a particular director will generally underestimate the time he will take to get a series of shots. In future you may either avoid using

that director or alternatively ensure that the budget is constructed to allow for the extra time. Experience may warn you that certain locations will incur additional expense because the subsistence costs of hotels and meals are more expensive at a certain time of year – again the choice might be to avoid the location or to budget for the additional costs.

4   **Exceed the overall budget**: Only in the most exceptional circumstances would you be prepared to do this, but it is a possibility. You should at least have an idea where the money will come from eventually. It might (depending on the production, of course) come from your own pocket; from any profit you are making from the programme, or you might negotiate an overspend from the commissioner or client (if you are lucky!). The worst thing you could do is to bury your head in the sand and like Mr Micawber simply hope that 'something will turn up'. This last route has, of course, been taken many times, and just as often, companies have gone bust.

On this happy note, perhaps it is now time to turn to the preliminary task of constructing the budget. You should not have to complete this task too often from scratch; you will soon discover the advantages of building a template or indeed a range of templates which will cater for a variety of different programme types or genres depending on the work of your production team or company. This, of course, implies that you will be using a computer program to help you to do this – usually a spreadsheet like OpenOffice *Calc*, which can be downloaded free of charge, or Microsoft *Excel*. This computerised approach using a spreadsheet is to be highly recommended. In this way you can build in calculations so you do not have to do them yourself, and if you make mistakes or need to make major or minor changes you can do so easily without starting over again. Perhaps most important is the fact that your spreadsheets can accommodate changes so that they come to reflect your experience of operating different budget heads or cost centres. I have heard the word *template* used by experienced Production Managers almost as often as I have heard them talk about *lists*! Experience is the stock-in-trade of the PM and templates are an excellent way of conserving and re-using this invaluable commodity.

> **Summary points – introduction to budgeting**
>
> - *Be prepared to be assertive*
> - *Write your contingency experiences back into future budgets*
> - *Make and use templates for your budgets*
> - *Be prepared to revise and modify templates*

Building a budget

There is no industry-wide template for budgets, though all programme budgets have certain elements in common. Most will divide the relevant cost centres between pre-production, production and post-production phases. This helps to break down the overall budgets into manageable sections and also provides a number of fixed points at which to assess the health or otherwise of current spending in budgetary terms. Film and drama genres will tend to make use of the terms *above-the-line* and *below-the line* costs. This sounds dauntingly grand but refers simply to those costs which are incurred before a project can begin. They are broadly connected with the development of the programme idea. Such costs may be incurred in securing the rights (for example, if a book is to be dramatised) and then for writers' fees and producers' salaries. In factual programming, this pre-production or above-the-line expenditure may include the costs of employing a researcher to develop the idea and to verify its viability in programming terms. The exact distribution of costs between above- and below-the-line costs might well vary from company to company and will often be determined largely by the commissioner of the programme, simply to ensure compatibility with the commissioner's accounting procedures.

What is a budget for?

This question may seem like an invitation to state the obvious, but it is worthwhile pondering the various purposes for which a budget may be constructed. Clearly a budget will provide a detailed list of all the items which need to be paid for, from morning coffee for the crew to licences to use music or excerpts from other programmes in the final production.

So the budget is a *check-list* of items, a reminder not only that items need to be paid for, but that arrangements need to be made and bookings confirmed. So the budget will include not only the costs of hiring camera equipment (if the company does not own its own kit) but also of paying facilities fees to those whose buildings or land are going to be 'borrowed' in the course of the production. A good check-list is a set of reminders of items, however small and apparently insignificant, which are vital to the programme and the smooth running of its production. Checking the costs of the item on 'tape costs', for example, will serve as a timely reminder to actually order the physical tapes that are required – so the budget itself may well generate a to-do list of items and tasks which need to be completed.

The budget allows the PM to *track*, or *monitor* costs as they arise, and therefore gives the ability to control such costs. In other words, in operation, the budget provides information which is vital for the programme to be completed in a cost-efficient manner.

A further important outcome of a carefully constructed budget is that it can be developed into a cash-flow statement showing when funds are required at each stage in the production. This cash flow will then be agreed between the funder and the producer.

In the following pages we are going to set about constructing a basic production budget for a factual programme with explanatory notes, where appropriate, on specific cost centres. It should be clear from the outset that the costs here are for illustration only, and do not claim to accurately reflect the sums that might have to be paid. The spreadsheet below is available to download from the web site associated with this book and may be modified for you to use for your own programmes.

The example budget is for a fairly simple factual programme such as a short 30-minute documentary. The pre-production period is two weeks, production shooting will be spread over six weeks and post production will last for just under two weeks.

It is important to keep checking the budget as you construct it to ensure that it complies fully with your intentions from the outset.

Pre-production

Figure 4.1 is part of a spreadsheet which gives a simple account of estimated pre-production (or *above-the-line*) costs and is for the most part self-explanatory.

◇	A	B	C	D	E
1	Budget outline – simple factual programme				
2			PLANNED COSTS		
3	Pre-production	Number	Unit	Cost	Total
4	1 Pre-production – story/script/development				
5	Story and script fee	1	1	£650	£650
6	Producer/director	1	week	£800	£800
7	Researcher	2	week	£500	£1,000
8	Pre-production sub-total				£2,450

Figure 4.1 Beginning a simple budget

Column A allows us to specify the main headings and cost centres. So in row 4 we refer to pre-production costs. Although it is not strictly necessary, it may be wise to number the cost centres as we have done here for ease of reference during discussion.

Columns B and C express units and costs, respectively. In this example, the one-off fee for script writing is shown in cell 5D. It is quite clear from this part of the spreadsheet that we have estimated or negotiated a weekly fee of £800 and £500, respectively, for the producer/director and for the researcher. The researcher is going to work for two weeks in the pre-production period, but the producer/director is budgeted for only one week.

Column E enables us to calculate the total for each part of the cost centre, and at cell E8 to keep a subtotal of the spend for pre-production. Remember that if we do not make an allowance for travel and subsistence at this stage, than we need to make sure that these expenses are covered later in the budget.

Production

The categories included in the production budget are numbered from 2–9 in the extract from the spreadsheet shown below. Before we look at each of these categories in detail it is worth noting that it is possible to represent each cost centre as a simple total with little detail. This could be regarded as a short-form budget and will be useful sometimes where what is required is a brief overview so that each area of expenditure can be quickly and easily located. Generally speaking, it is more useful in production terms to have a rather more detailed analysis, where each cost centre is broken down into a subset of categories, thus giving a far more detailed picture of exactly how the overall budget is allocated. The example budget for a simple factual programme uses a mixture of these two approaches, showing detail where it is likely to be helpful, and omitting it where it is not needed. Figure 4.2 lists projected expenditure for production categories 2–9.

Production staff category 2.1 covers the employment of a producer/ director. The number of weeks is set at six in cell B11 at a rate of £1,000 per week, and the total, £6,000, is calculated by the spreadsheet and shown in the total column at cell E11. You will note that although the weekly rate for a director is shown in D12, because there is no entry for the number of weeks in B12, no fee is shown in the total column. Because we are employing a versatile and talented producer/director we have no specific requirement for a director as such. This situation

◇	A	B	C	D	E
9	Production				
10	2.1 Producer/Director				
11	Producer	6	week	£1,000	£6,000
12	Director			£800	
13	2.2 Crew – camera				
14	Camera person	6	week	£1,000	£6,000
15	Camera assistant			£800	
16	2.3 Crew – sound				
17	Sound recordist	6	week	£800	£4,800
18	2.4 Crew – lighting				
19	Sparks			£650	
20	2.5 Crew – Production assistant				
21	Production assistant	6	week	£650	£3,900
22	3 Production equipment (hired)				
23	3.1 Camera	6	week	£500	£3,000
24	3.2 Sound kit				
25	3.3 Lighting kit				
26	4 Presenters/actors/talent				
27	4.1 Presenter	1	week	£2,000	£2,000
28	5 Tape stock				
29	5.1 Tapes	30	notional	£10	£300
30	5 Studio/locations	1	notional	£300	£300
31	6 Travel/transport				
32	Rate 53p per mile	600	per mile	£0.53	£318
33	7 Wardrobe/make-up/art department				
34	8 Hotels/living				
35	Lunch	150	per meal	£5	£750
36	Evening meal	50	per meal	£10	£500
37	Hotel/B&B	25	per night	£50	£1,250
38	9 Other expenses – specify				
39	E.g. petty cash on location	1	notional	£200	£200
40	Production sub-total				£29,318

Figure 4.2 A simple budget (production section)

is echoed in 2.2 where we have provided for a camera operator for the shoot but not for a camera assistant, although the weekly rate for the latter is shown on the budget spreadsheet. Similarly, on this production we do not plan to make use of a sparks (lighting electrician) on the crew, although again a weekly rate is shown. Incidentally, it is worth remembering that we could consider having a sparks on a one-off basis for a day or two. In such an eventuality, we would change cells C19 and D19 to show a daily rate instead of a weekly rate. For this example documentary however, we will leave the category with no entry. On balance it is probably better to leave these empty categories to stand on the budget template as occasions will no doubt arise in future where they are required. The main aim is to make the template as useful and flexible as possible without it being so simple as to be uninformative on the one hand, or overcomplicated and cumbersome on the other.

Production equipment (hired) allows for the fact that your production unit might well not own its own equipment, or that another crew is using it, in which case you might have to hire in what you need. It is worth remembering that you may not have to pay a full daily or weekly rate for such hires. Many companies will be willing to negotiate a deal if you propose to hire for longer periods. In such a case you might be able to obtain seven-days' worth of equipment hire for the price of five days, or six weeks for the price of five weeks. Again it might well be worth considering a package deal on your equipment hires. It might be cheaper to hire camera, sound and basic lighting from one supplier than to hire each item individually. If you do such a deal it is useful to note this at some appropriate place on your budget as a reminder of how you arrived at the cost estimate.

Presenters/actors/talent is the point in your budget where you account for the fees of those appearing in front of the camera. You might pay by the day simply for the days you call on a presenter. Alternatively you could agree a block fee for the production. You will, of course, carefully work out your call times so that you make best use of the talent in the time you have available. Most of these fees will be negotiated on a production-by-production basis, though you should be aware of agreements which have been negotiated by trade bodies such as PACT acting for independent producers and which are binding on their members.

Tape stock is a fairly self-explanatory category and can be adapted to allow for the costs of other methods of recording on location, such as the use of hard drives or solid state recording devices. You might wish to rename this category as 'consumables' and then provide sub-categories to specify what these are. This would be helpful on bigger and more complex productions where such items are significant in budgetary terms.

Studio/locations might well be an important factor in your budget. You may have no use for a studio, but you cannot expect to have free run of people's houses for example, without offering some monetary compensation for the disruption you will inevitably cause, however careful you intend to be. The same applies to the use of gardens or offices, or in scores of private places your camera operator and director may wish to use. You should not rely solely on the goodwill of proprietors, as you will need this irrespective of whether you pay a fee or not. Long gone are the days when members of the public were prepared to cooperate simply for the prestige of their property appearing on television; you might be lucky but do not depend on it.

Do not be too quick to dismiss the use of a studio. Such a facility might well be creatively advantageous as well as economically justified. Shooting against black or 'green-screen' in the controlled environment of a studio might save a great deal of location time and be visually more pleasing for interview situations. You will, of course, have to make a compensating budget allowance for bringing interviewees to your studio rather than taking the crew to them. This example may point up the consideration that what on the surface might seem to be an expensive option could in the end turn out to be quite economically attractive. This is also a good example of what could be a positive creative tension between the creative requirements and demands of the programme and the budget it has at its disposal.

Travel and transport could easily be forgotten but are often a vital part of the production and a significant element in the budget. The crew may well need to move from place to place and this has a significant cost. Depending on the details of your production, you may wish to add entries to allow you to specify hire costs of crew cars, public transport, air fares and so on. You may well also wish to specify a mileage rate for individuals' own vehicles. You should bear in mind that such use could have implications for insurance cover and that this situation needs to be investigated. Many of those working on your team might be covered on their own insurance to drive to and from work, but not *in the course* *of* work. Whatever the case, you need to be quite clear on this point. Another point which requires careful attention is the situation with VAT payments. Most travel and transport, buses, trains and air fares, for example, are zero-rated for VAT. Items such as car hire should not appear in this cost centre because they attract VAT at the current rate. There is a fuller discussion of this issue at the point where the VAT calculation is included towards the end of the budget.

Wardrobe/make-up/art department – a simple documentary programme may have no apparent requirement for expenditure under this heading. It is worth, however, reflecting on this assertion before moving on. If, for example, you are filming interviews under lights, you might need to consider the presence of a make-up artist. Similarly, if talent requires special equipment or clothing do you really expect them to provide this from their own pocket? This expectation might be quite justified if they are a climber, for example. In such a case you could be justified in expecting them to have and to use their own clothing, shoes, etc. The reasonable approach is to assume that the production will have to undertake any expense which is required as a result of the programme making. It is always a good idea for a film crew to carry some basic make-up such as tissues and face powder. Interviewees have the right not to appear to be hot, sweaty and uncomfortable on camera unless that is an integral part of the story you are filming. If you do buy such items, these belong in the consumables category.

Hotels and living accounts for the costs you will incur for any overnight stays for crew and talent. This can form a significant portion of the budget and you should take care to calculate this carefully. Five nights in a hotel costing £50 per room per night for a crew of five is going to cost $5 \times 5 \times 50$, a total of £1,250. If you make the simple mistake of allowing only 5×50 your budget will be in trouble very quickly! Overnight rates need to be carefully agreed in advance with your crew and talent, as do meal allowances. Again, remember that specific agreements may be in force with trade bodies such as PACT, BECTU or Equity and these should be observed.

Other expenses is a useful category for holding items which do not have a place anywhere else. As a catch-all it will be useful only if such items are specified, even if in a fairly general way. The heading should only cover relatively petty items. If this budget category becomes too large and all-inclusive, the information in your budget is compromised.

Post-production

◇	A	B	C	D	E
41	**Post-production**				
42	10.1 Producer/Director	3	weeks	£800	£2,400
43	10.2 Edit suite off-line (incl. editor)	10	days	£250	£2,500
44	10.3 Edit suite on-line (incl. editor)	2	days	£500	£1,000
45	11 Graphics	1	notional	£300	£300
46	12 Copyright clearance	1	notional	£300	£300
47	Post-production sub-total				£6,500

Figure 4.3 A simple budget (post-production section)

Post-production facilities include most obviously your editing costs, especially if you have to go to an outside editing facility. Here you may pay less for lower-resolution 'off-line' editing, and then move to a relatively short period for 'online' editing and conforming. You may also wish to expand this category to allow for audio dubbing facilities hire if you are adding commentary or you require a fairly sophisticated audio track.

Graphics – this category will help you to remember to budget for graphics for titles and credits if you need to commission these from outside companies.

Copyright clearance is one of the most important categories you deal with. Extracts from other works; books, films, other television programmes and music all need to be fully reported and paid for. All commissioners require evidence that your programme is fully compliant in this respect. You should always negotiate such fees as far as possible in advance. If you do not, your production may well be held up while negotiations are concluded. Lack of agreement at this stage may mean a re-edit so that the uncleared content is removed and replaced. Clearing material in retrospect or re-editing to remove it can prove to be disastrously expensive and has caused more than a few production companies to cease trading.

The bottom line

The tail-end of the budget sheet contains a number of important and significant elements before reaching the total production budget. These can be seen in Figure 4.4.

◇	A	B	C	D	E
48	**13 Office overheads**	1	notional	£3,500	£3,500
49	**14 Insurance**	1	notional	£2,500	£2,500
50	Admin and overheads sub-total				£6,000
51					
52	Total pre-production (above the line)				£2,450
53					
54	Total production/post-production (below the line)				£41,818
55					
56	Contingency				£4,427
57					
58	Production fee				£6,404
59					
60	VAT on all items excluding travel and transport				£9,587
61					
62	**Total production budget**				£64,686

Figure 4.4 A simple budget (the bottom line)

Office overheads are an important matter. A proportion of what it costs to run your office and pay your company bills needs to be borne by each production you undertake, and this is understood by commissioners. The level at which this is set may vary. The term 'notional' used here indicates that the amount is derived from an estimate based on experience and common practice rather than on a specific rate. It may be agreed with the commissioner that this figure represents a percentage of the total programme budget.

Production insurance cannot be overlooked and is required by commissioners. This insurance will cover many eventualities so that programme monies can be recovered in the case of serious situations arising which might jeopardise the completion of the project or cause substantial delays to it. Such situations might involve the death or injury of contributors or loss of or damage to footage or equipment. Specialist companies exist to undertake such insurance cover. Some details of such companies can be found in the reference section. Premiums are generally based on a percentage of the total production budget.

Contingency is an important safeguard in any budget, though it should not be used as a way to avoid paying detailed attention to your estimates in all the other categories. Essentially the contingency cost centre is an emergency fund and should be treated as such. Most Production Managers will do their utmost to avoid dipping into contingency and use it only as a last resort. At the same time, contingency is a way of recognising that at best the budget is simply a 'best estimate' of likely costs and that however carefully it is constructed there will be variations when it comes to actual expenditure.

Production fee is essentially the company 'profit' for making the programme and is set here at about 10 per cent of the total budget. Commissioners will have strict guidelines for agreeing a production fee.

VAT (value added tax) is the final item before the bottom-line calculation. You will have to pay VAT on all your purchases apart from certain items such as travel and transport and these have been specifically excluded from the formula which calculates the VAT element on our budget spreadsheet. If you are registered for VAT you will be able to reclaim the VAT element on your purchases but will have to charge VAT to your clients (and, of course, account to HMRC for what you have received). You will be able to obtain specific information and guidance from your local VAT office about the level of turnover at which you must register, and how you must keep your company books. Advice given here is of necessity brief. You will be well advised to seek expert help from your accountant if you think you might be liable to register for VAT.

Total production budget – congratulations, you have now reached the 'bottom line' of your budget, though sadly I have to tell you that your work may not yet be over. Most commissioners will have set a 'guide-price' for commissions of a particular genre and of a certain length. Having reached a budget of nearly sixty-five thousand pounds for our documentary may mean that it is too expensive for the commissioner. It could, of course, also be on the cheap side! Having constructed your preliminary budget, you may have to rethink your costs. It may well be that you can pull back your filming. Six weeks is, after all, quite generous. The good news is that having set up your budget on a spreadsheet, it is simplicity itself to change it and to see the effect on your overall budget virtually instantly.

Managing the budget

Having created your budget, then checked it and had it accepted, there remains the ongoing task of managing it. To do this you need continuing information. Essentially you now embark on one of production management's most important tasks, that of tracking the budget. If you receive a late evening telephone call from your crew on location asking 'can we manage an extra day's care hire?', for example, you need to be able to provide an answer fairly quickly. Your original spreadsheet budget will, of course, tell you what you had estimated for this particular cost centre. It will not, however, tell you how much of this budget you have already spent. For this purpose you will need budget reports. These can, of course, be quite sophisticated and detailed but for our purposes we can build a tracking system onto our original budget spreadsheet so that we will not have to repeat all our painstaking groundwork. By adding extra columns to our spreadsheet and furnishing them with the right calculations we can track how much we have spent, what is left of the budget and how far, in percentage terms, we have deviated from our plans. Again you may, if you wish, download a copy of a second spreadsheet which includes reporting functions from the web site associated with this book.

Budget reports

Figure 4.5 on the following page shows that our original budget figures and cost centres in columns B–E have now been headed 'planned costs'. Further columns have been added alongside to indicate how much of the planned budget has been spent in total so far (column H), what percentage this represents of the total allocated under this cost centre (column G) and most importantly, what is left of this total and is therefore still available to be spent (column I). On the *live* spreadsheet available online, you will find that this column conveniently highlights overspends in red, and shows amounts which are still available in green. In essence, the area of the spreadsheet from columns A–I will represent our budget report – what we started with and what we have left – accounting for every item in our original costing. This report may be produced as often as required and provides a statement or snapshot of the state of the budget at any given time. The wise will, of course, recognise that a report will only be as accurate as the information it contains. Ensuring regular and accurate input of information is the next step in running our budget.

◇	A	B	C	D	E	F	G	H	I	J	K	L
1	Budget outline – simple factual programme											
2			PLANNED COSTS				ACTUAL PRODUCTION SPENDING			P Ord. No.		
3	Pre-production	Number	Unit	Cost	Total		% Spent	Total spent	Available	or date	Amount	
4	1 Pre-production – story/script/development											
5	Story and script fee	1	1	£650	£650		100%	£ 650.00	£ -	132	£ 650.00	
6	Producer/director	1	week	£800	£800		100%	£ 800.00	£ -	133	£ 800.00	
7	Researcher	2	week	£500	£1,000		50%	£ 500.00	£ 500.00	135	£ 500.00	
8	Pre-production sub-total				£2,450		80%	£ 1,950.00	£ 500.00			
9	Production											
10	2.1 Producer/Director											
11	Producer	6	week	£1,000	£6,000		80%	£ 4,800.00	£ 1,200.00	134	£ 4,800.00	
12	Director			£800								
13	2.2 Crew – camera											
14	Camera person	6	week	£1,000	£6,000		80%	£ 4,800.00	£ 1,200.00	123	£ 4,800.00	
15	Camera assistant			£800								
16	2.3 Crew – sound											
17	Sound recordist	6	week	£800	£4,800		63%	£ 3,000.00	£ 1,800.00	124	£ 3,000.00	
18	2.4 Crew – lighting											
19	Sparks			£650								
20	2.5 Crew – Production assistant											
21	Production assistant	6	week	£650	£3,900			£ -	£ 3,900.00			
22	3 Production equipment (hired)											
23	3.1 Camera	6	week	£500	£3,000			£ -	£ 3,000.00			
24	3.2 Sound kit											
25	3.3 Lighting kit											
26	4 Presenters/actors/talent											
27	4.1 Presenter	1	week	£2,000	£2,000		115%	£ 2,300.00	-£ 300.00	121	£ 2,300.00	
28	5 Tape stock											
29	5.1 Tapes	30	notional	£10	£300			£ -	£ 300.00			
30	5 Studio/locations	1	notional	£300	£300			£ -	£ 300.00			
31	6 Travel/transport											
32	Rate 53p per mile	600	per mile	£0.53	£318			£ -	£ 318.00			
33	7 Wardrobe/make-up/art department											
34	8 Hotels and living											
35	Lunch	150	per meal	£5	£750			£ -	£ 750.00			
36	Evening meal	50	per meal	£10	£500			£ -	£ 500.00			
37	Hotel/B&B	25	per night	£50	£1,250			£ -	£ 1,250.00			
38	9 Other expenses – specify											
39	E.g. petty cash on location	1	notional	£200	£200			£ -	£ 200.00			
40	Production sub-total				£29,318		51%	£ 14,900.00	£ 14,418.00			

Figure 4.5 Budget reports

Keeping the budget up to date with purchase orders

Referring to Figure 4.5 above, you will see that further columns, K and L have been added to our sheet. In fact two more pairs M and N, O and P have been added too, but there is no room for them on the printed page; they do, however, figure in the online version. These columns allow you to input amounts you spend as you spend them. There are two important recommendations as to how you might achieve this. The first is that you operate a system of *purchase orders*. Purchase orders are an essential way of controlling and tracking your budgets.

A numbered purchase order signed by the Production Manager or other designated person should be the only authorised way of committing production budgets, other than on crewing and wages. The introduction of such a system is to be highly recommended. Consequently it is vital that every member of the production team is aware that the system is in place and how it is to be operated. This means also that there will need to be a clear understanding of the monetary limits of petty cash purchases and what these are.

The system will run smoothly if every item of expenditure has its own purchase order. This means that as soon as you are committed to spending a sum of money you issue a purchase order and enter that in the appropriate

HYPOTHETICAL PRODUCTIONS LTD
21 Tripod Street Bristol XXX XXX
Tel. 1234 5678

Production Manager	Production title	Producer/Director
Sam Smith Mob. 01111 22222		Jo Brown Mob. 02222 33333

Official purchase order

To: Name of Supplier

Address Line 1

Address Line 2

Address line 3

Postcode

Date

Purchase Order Number:

Dear _____

Please supply the following items/services:

Signed_____

(Authorised signatory)

Please ensure that the above purchase order number is quoted on all invoices

Figure 4.6 A sample purchase order form

column, K for the Purchase Order Number, and L for the amount you are committed to. Thus, for instance, if you have just booked the hire of some kit for the shoot, you should enter that information immediately in your purchases columns (K and L). The beauty of the purchase order system is that it allows you to enter the spending as soon as you are committed to it. This avoids the embarrassment of spending your allocation under a particular cost centre, and then finding a late invoice from a purchase you had forgotten.

Alternatively, if this is too complicated an operation, and your production unit is small, you could gather your expenditure on a weekly basis and enter the date into column K rather than the purchase order number. If you adopt this system though, you will need to be very thorough in the way you keep track, not only of what you have spent, but expenditure you are committed to at some future point.

A further recommendation is that as soon as you start your spreadsheet you enter all items that you are contracted for, such as freelance crew costs. You may not have purchase orders for such items, but you are committed, and entering such known costs immediately will prevent you issuing a report which indicates vast swathes of your budget as underspent when in reality it is already as good as spent!

Summary points – budgeting

- *Your budget template should contain a useful level of detail – but not become too complicated!*
- *Remember that you can make deals with crew and equipment hire costs – budgets should show the details*
- *You might need a category for consumables when such items are significant in budgetary terms*
- *From time to time apparently expensive solutions (such as using a studio) might turn out to be economically attractive – it is always worth investigating*
- *Take care where you include items which carry no VAT – these should be shown separately*
- *Remember that certain rates, such as expenses and overnights, will be subject to agreements in force with trade bodies and trades unions or associations*
- *Negotiations for the use of copyright material should be undertaken as soon as possible and always before it is incorporated into the production*
- *Wherever possible use purchase orders as a way of keeping control of production spending*

5
Creating and managing schedules

Quick start definitions

Schedule: a list containing information about times and locations for shooting specific sections of the programme

Call-sheet: a document outlining the times various members of the production are required on location or on set

Contact-sheet: a document containing relevant contact information for each member of the crew and cast so they can be contacted as and when required

Post: often used to shorten the term 'post-production'

Recce: literally to reconnoitre in order to assess the suitability of and gain information about proposed locations, etc.

Introduction

Scheduling is at the heart of the production management role, looking after the day-to-day running of the project. Once again we will be able to make use of lists and templates in order to begin to put together schedules so that the production can be managed efficiently and coherently. Again, the strong recommendation would be to use a spreadsheet. This kind of computer software enables the creation of documents which are very simple, and yet capable of development into spreadsheets of great sophistication and complexity. This flexibility is invaluable in the work of the Production Manager, as is the ability to develop a template as the need arises without having to start the work over again from scratch. The templates used as examples in this chapter are available for download and may be adapted to your own particular requirements. One of the outstanding advantages of the use of spreadsheets in this context is that they can serve as a central gathering place for all the practical information needed for scheduling and can be updated as details fall into place when, for example, locations are confirmed and arrangements are made. A central spreadsheet for this information can also be used to generate other documents, such as call sheets and contact sheets, as they are required. As in earlier chapters, we will look first at scheduling for a simple factual programme and then go on to see how the basic principles are applied in drama, again at a fairly simple level.

Creating a schedule

Much if not all of the information you need to start building your schedule is to be found in the budget. You will have been supplied with an agreed programme budget; indeed you may well have played a major part in its origination. Without an agreed budget, you will not be in any position to start making proposals and decisions about scheduling. The reasons for this assertion are fairly obvious. Without agreed parameters for the length of the shoot and the amount of time devoted to post-production (editing, graphics preparation and sound dubbing for example), it is impossible to begin to construct a production schedule.

The Production Manager needs time to sit down with the director and producer to agree how the allocated budgets can be expressed in terms of the time to be allocated to various activities. We will base our schedule construction on the budget we set up in the previous chapter. As in all matters of programme production, we will be wise to base all our work on the three production periods, pre-production, production and post-production (the last often referred to simply as 'post'). The discussion with the senior members of the production team takes place not in order to change what has been allocated in the budget, but to agree how resources are to be deployed.

Pre-production

The pre-production budget (page 35) reveals that the researcher is on board for two weeks and that the producer/director (often referred to as

The recce – an important detour!

It costs a great deal of money to have a production crew *'on the road'*. Just how *much* it costs can be crudely calculated by dividing the production budget of crew, transport and all the other associated costs by the number of days allocated for the shoot. Whatever the particular result of this calculation, the conclusion will inevitably be that this is an expensive exercise! It stands to reason that any production company will be anxious to ensure that the best possible use is made of every day and every hour of a crew's time.

The efficient use of a crew's time can only be assured if shooting days are well planned. The term 'recce' (pronounced *rekki*) is in common use in the film and television industries and describes the exercise of scoping, scouting or seeing how the land lies. Simple though this seems, there are a number of important and not always obvious elements which go to make up a thorough and useful recce.

Visually the location needs to be right, to say the 'right' things in terms of the subject so that possibly irrelevant (and therefore distracting) detail can be easily avoided in the way the shot is framed. Seeing the location at the relevant time of day might also be crucial. That particularly effective shot might not be available when the sun is in the wrong direction. Try not to recce a location in the morning if you intend to shoot in the evening! Recce-ing at the right time of day might avoid embarrassing mistakes too, when for instance a local school finishes for the day just as you are trying to shoot a quiet sequence!

Acoustically the location also needs to be checked. Can any distracting sound be eliminated or controlled for example?

Practically there may be important, if prosaic, considerations to be taken into account. Whatever the size of crew they will need to eat; are there facilities, if not will you be able to cater on location? Comfort breaks are important too; are toilets and washing facilities within reasonable reach? Can your crew park vehicles without difficulty? If you need to use lighting and no power is available you may have to provide (and pay for) mobile generators.

Are permissions likely to be given for use of the location? However suitable it may be in all other respects, if you anticipate difficulties it may be wiser to choose another place.

Even a cursory consideration of these points reveals just what a devastating impact a lack of care in the recce, or worst of all, omitting it altogether can have on both budget and schedule, and how easily you can *blow a hole* in both!

the PD) will be working for one week in this period. Assuming that these resources have not been allocated in a random way, we may conclude that the thinking is that the researcher will have a clear week for preliminary research on the availability of interviewees and suitable locations. After that first week, the researcher will be joined by the producer/director who will lead the *recce* from a creative point of view. The PD will want to verify not only the practicality of the proposed arrangements, but the creative possibilities they offer the programme for which he or she will be responsible.

Strictly speaking, the recce is outside the scope of a book focused on production management. The recce is an essential part of the pre-production process. It is often undervalued and consequently neglected, especially by the less experienced. Because an inadequate recce can have a devastating impact on both the budget and schedule of any programme, it seems worth a pause at this point to consider in greater depth the value of a well-conducted recce. With no apologies, the 'Recce' box (page 49) provides just a few points to reinforce the importance of this prudent exercise of foresight and planning.

Preparations

During the recce, information will be gathered to enable the Production Manager to work on the detail of the schedule so that as facts are gathered and strategy is planned, the details can be added. At this stage, it does not really matter if precise dates are not yet available. This is the beauty of the spreadsheet. You may well start by allocating your time into weeks with no dates at all. Then as dates do become available you can add these to your schedule. Next you will be gathering more detailed information which may well enable you to break down your shooting weeks into specific days, and finally to add the dates to those days.

So if you are using a spreadsheet, you might start with a very simple outline, as shown in Figure 5.1. Here we have simply transferred the information from the budget and shown pre-production, production and post-production weeks on a simple form. At this stage it is probably better not to show the weeks running from 1 to 10 but to restart the numbering afresh for each production period. For sound reasons (like availability) production may not flow immediately after the pre-production period.

HYPOTHETICAL PRODUCTIONS LTD 21 Tripod Street Bristol XXX XXX Tel. 1234 5678				
Production Manager		Production title		Producer/Director
Sam Smith Mob. 01111 22222				Jo Brown Mob. 02222 33333
Pre-production		Location details		Useful information
Week 1 Researcher only		Local 3 days, city 2 days		
Week 2 Researcher and Producer/Director		TBA		
Production				
Week 1		Local filming		
Week 2				
Week 3				
Week 4				
Week 5				
Week 6		Liverpool filming		
Post-production				
Week 1 off-line (5 days)		Quick Cuts edit facility		Booked and
Week 2 off-line (5 days)		Editor (Tony)		confirmed
Week 3 on-line (2 days)		Conform Edit, London Road		Confirmed – Editor tba

Figure 5.1 A simple schedule outline

In some circumstances it might be wise to build in a planning pause between the two, so that there is time for permissions to be arranged and facilities fees negotiated before committing to shooting in a particular location.

It is quite clear that at this stage the information contained in the schedule is fairly minimal. Note though that some broad outline information has been inserted. We have decided, for example, that in week 1 of production (row 11 of the spreadsheet) filming is to be local and that in week 6 we are travelling further afield to shoot in Liverpool. Note also that we have also booked our editing facilities (rows 43–46), probably because we need to ensure that the facilities will be available to us exactly when we need them.

So far, the schedule is self-explanatory, and can easily be expanded to include more detailed information when it becomes available. There is absolutely no reason why a Production Manager who is reasonably adept at manipulating and working with spreadsheets should not set up a number of 'hidden' columns which will not be printed or made available to others. Such columns might contain notes of contact numbers and other details which are not required by all the members of the production team.

Production and post-production

Our example budget provides for six weeks of location shooting. Few if any documentaries will have a prepared script, although by this stage the producer/director will have a number of locations in mind. Some of these will be essential; others will be desirable, so already there is the possibility of prioritising the shooting schedule. Other genres of factual programming may well have a fixed formula. Much 'reality' programming follows pre-set formats and each programme in the series will follow a similar schedule with a fresh set of dates and perhaps only minor deviations from the set pattern as circumstances demand. In such cases the same budget and schedule templates will be used over and over again with minor changes to schedules as are required.

It is clear from the agreed budget that virtually all the location shooting will be on home ground. The travel and transport budget is extremely modest and certainly does not envisage foreign trips. If this were the case then the cost of air fares and ferries, special insurance and other items would be clearly shown. The fact that only six hundred miles are budgeted for means that over six weeks of shooting mileage will have to be very low indeed. While this hypothetical situation is unlikely, it is perfectly possible. It might, for example, be that four or even five weeks' filming will take place in the immediate vicinity of the production office, and only in the last week or two would the crew venture further afield.

From the revised spreadsheet in Figure 5.2, we can quickly see that there have been developments and that these have been easily incorporated into the spreadsheet by expanding the rows where necessary. Filming has been arranged for the first two days and details have been noted on the spreadsheet. The vigilant reader will, however, have noticed that the information was already present in the previous table, but was hidden. You will see in Figure 5.2 that the row numbering jumps from 11 to 38. These hidden rows have now been completed and revealed in the subsequent development of our schedule spreadsheet. At the same time, additional detailed information has been added as it became available. Telephone numbers and agreed timings have been added, and these will prove invaluable when we come to construct our call sheets. This is a further illustration of how a single spreadsheet can serve several purposes and might well, on fairly simple productions, be more than adequate as a production planning and management tool.

HYPOTHETICAL PRODUCTIONS LTD 21 Tripod Street Bristol XXX XXX Tel. 1234 5678				
Production Manager		Production title		Producer/Director
Sam Smith Mob. 01111 22222				Jo Brown Mob. 02222 33333
Pre-production		Location details		Useful information
Week 1 Researcher only		Local 3 days, city 2 days		
Week 2 Researcher and Producer/Director		TBA		
Production				
Week 1		Local filming		
Mon 1 Sep		Interview D. Williams	AM	Phone 0112 3456
Crew rv on site 09.30, presenter 10.00		13 Burnfield View TL12 7PP		
Lunch				
Crew rv Bull's Head 13.45		GVs local area	PM	
Tues 2 Sep		Brewery shoot	AM	Contact – Manager 0222 3456
		Industrial estate ZY99 3YZ		
Lunch				
Crew/presenter call 14.00		Interview Mrs Ross	PM	Presenter required
		52 Hops Close ZY99 7YZ		
Wed 3 Sep		Interview Chief Constable	AM	Contact secretary
Crew/presenter call 09.00		Police HQ		0222 999 999
Lunch				
Crew call 13.30		GVs incident room		Contact duty sergeant
		Police HQ		name tb notified

Figure 5.2 A more detailed schedule

Learning from mistakes!

At this point it is worth noting the importance of ensuring that all the individuals working on the programme have been correctly allocated across the whole production period. For example, the producer/director needs to be properly contracted for the post-production editing period to ensure that there is someone present to supervise the edit! I should confess at this stage that in preparing the sample budget for the previous chapter, I failed to include a cost for the producer/director in the post-production section at expense item number 10 (see Figure 4.3, p 40). Having budgeted a 10-day off-line and a 2-day online edit, the producer/director will need to be present to supervise the edit for at least two-and-a-half working weeks. A three-week post-production period for the PD would not therefore be unreasonable and so I corrected the original budget accordingly. Once again the great advantage of working with templates is demonstrated. Once the correction is made to the spreadsheet, it stands as a reminder in all future budgets which come to be based on that template.

It will be clear from the way in which it has been possible to expand the detail contained in our original schedule template, that it will be quite easy to use this template to generate daily or weekly schedules as they are required. As I suggested earlier, it is worth taking advantage of the ability to hide rows and columns at will in order only to display information for a particular purpose. In this way, a simple scheduling operation can be prepared on a spreadsheet page which can then develop into what is in effect a whole project planning tool in the hands of the Production Manager.

Summary points – scheduling

The programme budget is the starting point for the schedule, you cannot start without it!

Call-sheet: a document outlining the times various members of the production team are required on location or on set

Contact-sheet: a document containing relevant contact information for each member of the crew and cast so they can be contacted as and when required

---

Scheduling for drama

> A rule says 'You must do it this way'. A principle says 'This works . . . and has through all remembered time'.
>
> McKee R (1997) *Story*, Regan Books

While most of the preceding parts of this chapter will be relevant to all genres of programme making, there are a number of skills and techniques which are the special requirements of drama or feature production. At first glance, scheduling a drama or feature shoot can appear an arcane and difficult, not to say a complicated mission. While it is true that you need the discipline to undertake a painstaking task (and as we shall see later there are tools which can streamline this process) the whole business takes us right back to the basic building blocks of the Production Manager's expertise – the list. Breaking down a script to construct a shooting schedule and all the ancillary items (such as call sheets) that go with it, is essentially compiling a list; even through it is a relatively complex and sophisticated list, it is still a list! In the following pages we will look a little more closely at the process of moving from a writer's script to a production schedule, which will help us to turn that script into a drama which can be shot efficiently.

Quick start definitions

Breakdown or script breakdown: the process of analysing a script and 'breaking it down' into its constituent parts

Department: A distinctive discipline or expertise within a production, for example, set building, wardrobe

Production Board: A physical, wall-mounted board holding coloured strips of paper corresponding to each scene in a feature and containing information relevant to it

Production Strip: See above – the actual physical strip of paper containing information about that scene

Recce: A reconnoitre, a visit in order to evaluate a proposed location.

The script is the starting point. It will usually (and preferably) be delivered with a minimum of 'direction' but will consist of dialogue and locations together with key descriptions of characters and essential props and other vital detail. A moment's thought will quickly lead to the conclusion that this script is not the document that will enable you to shoot the movie. Why not? In the first (and probably most important) place the script naturally follows the logical progression of the narrative or story as created by the writer. Locations may be visited and revisited and visited yet again by our characters in the course of the unfolding drama. This then is just one reason for changing the 'shooting order' so that scenes in the same location and similar times of day are shot together. In this way, crew travel and set-up time will be used more efficiently. If we begin to apply similar logic to other elements in our production, such as the use we make of our principal actors, expensive props (hired vehicles, for example) special effects, lighting and stunts, there should be little further need to justify a more analytical assessment of the script before we even think of putting film or tape in the camera. The next stage consists therefore of a rather more systematic approach to the script.

Script breakdown is the term used to describe such a systematic analysis of the script and its requirements. A standard way in which to achieve this breakdown was developed by the Hollywood film industry many years ago, and although the methods used to achieve this analysis have developed over the years, in essence little has changed. It is a tried and tested way and (to return to our quote from McKee, above) 'this works and has through all remembered time'. Little point then in attempting to devise a new system. The following step-by-step guide is offered as a simple version of this time-honoured method of script breakdown:

1   Ensure that your script is laid out in the standard format which will then enable you to adopt the conventional method of 'measuring' the length of each scene (see step 3 below). This book is not intended to provide a guide to writing and presenting screenplays and so I do not propose to elaborate on the details of standard script layout. It is, however, important to note that there are such standards. They may vary slightly (for example, the US standard page is known as 'letter', the corresponding European standard is 'A4'). Font sizes too are standardised. Further details are easily obtained from an Internet search. There are a number of commercial software packages which can help you to lay out scripts in standard format, and details are provided in the reference section of this book. It is also worth pointing out that Celtx (www.celtx.com) is a free integrated software program which enables you to write screenplays as well as to achieve other important goals as you break down your script.

2   Divide the script into scenes if this has not already been done. A scene will generally consist of action which takes place in a particular location or within a particular time frame. When that location or time changes, the scene changes. Each scene should be carefully numbered and the number adhered to throughout the process.

3   Measure the approximate length of each scene according to its 'page count'. This is achieved by dividing each page into eighths. In the film industry the standard script page consists of eight inches so that a scene which lasts just over a page can be described as 1 and 1/8 pages long. This can be a very good 'rule of thumb' measurement to help calculate the length of a scene for scheduling purposes.

4   Analyse the script scene by scene by identifying every element or component in the scene. This is the heart of the script breakdown and is very important in identifying everything that is required in order to shoot the scene. By element or component we mean actor, location (day or night), prop, vehicle, stunt and so on. Generally each element is colour coded to make its later identification simple and foolproof. The following table gives the industry standard colour codes for script breakdown. You may simplify the list and not use all the codes, but it is to be recommended that you retain the standard colour for each element you do identify.

Standard colour codes for script breakdown (elements)

- *CAST* – Red (speaking roles)
- *EXTRAS* – Yellow (Silent roles)
- *EXTRAS* – Green (Crowds and atmosphere)
- *STUNTS* – Orange
- *SPECIAL EFFECTS* – Blue
- *SOUND EFFECTS* – Brown
- *VEHICLES* – Pink
- *PROPS* – Purple
- *WARDROBE* – Circled
- *MAKE-UP AND HAIR* – Asterisk *
- *SPECIAL EQUIPMENT* – Boxed

---

5   Give a number to each character in your script. The conventional way is to assign the number 1 to the role with the most scenes, then number 2 to the next most scenes and so on. This numbering should then be consistently observed in all subsequent documents and schedules.

6   This systematic and colour-coded information can now be transferred to separate breakdown sheets (one for each scene). An example of a breakdown sheet follows below and can be downloaded from this book's web site. You should note that a further colour-coding scheme

is used for each scene, with a separate colour denoting the type and time of day of the location.

Standard colour coding for script breakdown (locations)

- *DAY Exterior* – Yellow
- *NIGHT Exterior* – Green
- *DAY Interior* – White
- *NIGHT Interior* – Blue

The script breakdown sheet enables all the elements contained within a particular scene to be brought together onto a single sheet; these sheets can then be used as a basis for making colour-coded strips for a traditional production board where coloured strips represent each scene. In this way, similar requirements can be grouped together so that the shoot is scheduled in a coherent and resource efficient manner.

It is undoubtedly helpful and worthwhile to become familiar with the traditional method of script breakdown and scheduling for drama features. Colour coded pens and strips of coloured paper mounted on wall boards are the tried and tested ways of arriving at a cross plot. A cross plot is simply another way of expressing a script by re-arranging the order of scenes into a viable and efficient running order for the shooting schedule. Only by breaking down the script in the way described above can this be arrived at. Fortunately computer software is now available to make this task rather easier and less demanding of assorted pens and strips of paper. Possibly the most well-known of these program packages is Movie Magic (www.screenplay.com) which plausibly claims to be the industry (meaning of course Hollywood) standard. There are other such offerings available, and some of these are listed in the reference section. A helpful alternative to commercial software is Celtx (www.celtx.com), an integrated software suite designed and maintained by a community of developers and users. Happily this software is free to download and use, and the blogs and forums associated with it provide useful advice, although the interface is helpful and intuitive. The program combines virtually all the pre-production elements of scriptwriting storyboarding

HYPOTHETICAL PRODUCTIONS LTD 21 Tripod Street Bristol xxx xxx Tel. 1234 5678		
Production Manager Sam Smith Mob. 01111 22222	Production title	Producer/Director Jo Brown Mob. 02222 33333
Scene #		Breakdown page #
Script page #	INT ☐ or ☐ EXT	
Page count	DAY ☐ or ☐ NIGHT	
Scene description		
Location		
Cast (red)	Extras – silent roles (yellow)	Props/weapons (purple)
	Extras – crowds/atmos (green)	Vehicles/animals (pink)
Special effects (blue)	Wardrobe (circle)	Make-up/hair (asterisk)
Special equipment (boxed)	Stunts (orange)	SFX/music (brown)

Figure 5.3 Example of a script breakdown sheet

and script breakdown with an impressive range of reports. The fact that it comes at no cost will no doubt endear it to those tasked with production management of many projects, as its templates are engineered to address the needs of feature film, documentary, audiovisual and radio drama among other production genres.

Especially useful is the ability to produce schedules from the same program interface and then to print them out as reports.

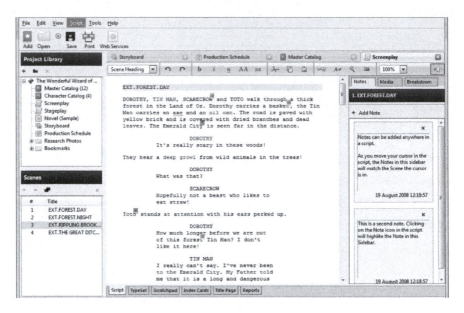

Figure 5.4 Script breakdown using Celtx

6
Managing Health and Safety

Quick start definitions

H&S: Health and Safety

Risk Assessment: A careful and documented consideration of what could cause harm to people

Competent person: A person with the relevant skills, training and experience to undertake a particular task

I would always approach [Health and Safety] by looking at the worst-case scenario and then try to make sure this doesn't happen, especially when it comes to risk assessments for filming.

Introduction

In this chapter we will consider the reasons why Health and Safety issues figure so large in the everyday work of production management. We will then go on to an examination of the basic steps which need to be undertaken in a risk assessment. After a more detailed look at the practical operation of a sound Health and Safety strategy within the production unit or organisation, this chapter concludes with an example of a simple form to record risk assessment activity.

Health and Safety is an important element in production management, not simply for the commonsense motive of eliminating or reducing the risk of harm, pain and suffering, but also because it is subject to various regulations imposed on employers by the law. This book should not be considered as any kind of guide to the law. I am not a lawyer, nor am I an expert in Health and Safety. This chapter is offered as an introduction to some of the principles and concerns that anyone involved in television production management will deal with. There is no substitute for experienced advice from experts, and training should be thought of as an essential constituent in your approach to Health and Safety matters.

It is fashionable to decry the increasing obsession in many areas of our lives with Health and Safety issues. At times it may seem as if professionally and personally we are hedged about with restrictions on our freedom and our creativity, all in the name of Health and Safety. Citing safety issues can, of course, be used as an excuse for avoiding difficult and complex situations which would otherwise require energy and application. No wonder then that in some areas Health and Safety has earned itself a reputation for petty bureaucracy and so easily provokes a certain exasperated expression and rolling of the eyes. Much of this reaction is unwarranted and unfair. As members of the public we all expect to be protected from hazards of any kind and are quick to criticise, complain and even to sue when things go wrong.

In such circumstances it is hardly surprising that Health and Safety plays such a large part in production management and in the lives of Production Managers. Not a single Production Manager failed to talk at length about Health and Safety during my research for this book. Such conversation was often accompanied by exasperated looks and sighs of frustration. I should quickly point out that the reason for such irritation was not the subject of safety in itself, but an expression of the uphill struggle encountered by many Production Managers when trying to ensure that all members of the production team complied, complainingly or not, with the required measures. No one, of course, welcomes work which may be time-consuming, tedious and repetitive and which, at worst, can seem only remotely relevant to the creative task at hand.

Even a moment's reflection, however, will remind us that being on location with a production crew can be a dangerous occupation full of potential and actual hazard. Most crews work under pressure; this pressure might be creative (to frame the right shots, find the appropriate sound) but it will doubtless also be about time (to achieve creative excellence in the shortest possible period). Working under pressure of any kind may mean that we are less aware of possible danger than we might otherwise be.

This then is the principal reason that Health and Safety issues must be taken seriously in production at any level.

Our concern with Health and Safety is not simply for our own health and well-being. Much production work involves working with or near members of the public. Many years ago I was working with a small video crew in a huge concert venue. Our aim was to demonstrate the technical and logistical aspects of the venue rather than to record the rock concert. But we needed to show the size of the crowd and the complexity of the technical rig and to do this we had to climb high under the roof of the building. In order to get the best shots we made our way over various catwalks. I do not find working at such height in the least agreeable, so I am naturally aware of the obvious dangers of such a situation. We were, however, well provided with safety rails. What I had failed to appreciate, however, was that between the catwalk and the handrail was open space, so that anything we put down for a few moments while we were shooting could so easily have fallen onto the crowd below. From that height, even a small item such as a spare camera battery would have killed anyone who might have been hit on the head.

This account illustrates a number of essential points. First, as a working crew we have a responsibility not only for ourselves, but for anyone around us who might be put at risk by our activity. Second, we can easily find ourselves in a situation which is fraught with dangers that we had simply not anticipated. At the time that this particular situation arose, little formal attention was paid to Health and Safety issues and certainly no prior risk assessment was completed on behalf of the production, although I hasten to add that commonsense precautions were always taken with a view to minimising risk. It is far less likely that in today's more risk-aware context such a situation would arise. That this is so should be celebrated; we have our obsession with Health and Safety to thank for a much improved safety record in our industry. A further point we might also bear in mind is that a vivid imagination is a valuable asset; if you can see the dangers in your mind's eye then you have made a good start on minimising the risks such dangers may pose.

The purpose of this introduction is to ensure that our approach to Health and Safety is rooted and remains rooted in a genuine concern for the well-being of all the members of the production team and anyone else with whom they might come into contact. Placing a toolbag on the pavement of a busy street while adjusting a tripod might so easily cause someone else to trip and fall. Elderly people often do not survive broken hips.

I am often amazed by how unaware groups can be of the impact they have on others in their vicinity. How are people to make their way to do their shopping when the pavement ahead is blocked by a film crew about their business? The likelihood is that they will step off the pavement to avoid the crew, and because they are interested in the antics of the sound recordist, they will probably not pay full attention to the traffic that is roaring by just inches away. Moments of inattention and lack of awareness are probably far more likely to cause accidents than major and well understood risks when shooting in obviously hazardous conditions.

It should be understood that the observations and suggestions which follow are pointers and suggestions for the way in which your approach to safety might be observed, improved and monitored. I make no claim to be an expert in Health and Safety and seek to follow the guidelines set out by the experts and those responsible for ensuring that we comply with the law. I will make suggestions for training and give information about the availability of such courses and I strongly urge that serious consideration be given to regular training in this area. Broadcasters and larger production companies will have policies in place to ensure compliance with Health and Safety legislation and will only commission from those who can demonstrate their own systems for compliance. My concern for the moment is with smaller and less experienced units, such as student productions and start-ups or small production companies, where formal training may be less well established and rigorous.

Making a start

At the simplest and most basic level, the Health and Safety Executive (HSE) (www.hse.gov.uk) proposes a five-step plan. This plan is available as a document to download, and information on how to contact the HSE is provided in the reference section. The five-step plan is essentially the framework for a simple risk assessment, but the principles it outlines lie at the heart of all Health and Safety procedures. The headings used here are based on suggestions outlined by the Health and Safety Executive:

Step 1 Look for hazards

This should be a physical inspection of the area of work, such as a shooting location. It should also include equipment which might be used. Looking for hazards might well also include using experience and imagination in order to anticipate hazardous situations.

Step 2 Decide who might be harmed

An essential step in risk assessment is to determine not only *what* the hazards are, but *who* might be at risk from them. Remember that you are not only concerned with your production team, but with anyone else with whom you come into contact.

Step 3 Evaluate the risk

This is the point at which you decide how serious the risk might be from a particular hazard, and what steps can be taken to do two things. At best the aim is to *avoid* the risk completely, if this is not possible, then what steps can be taken to *reduce* the risk as far as possible? This is also the point at which you might need to take action. This could include the provision of safety equipment, possibly training for those involved and certainly the implementation of systems and methods to facilitate the avoidance or reduction of risk.

Step 4 Record your findings

It is always good practice to keep a record of your findings, and the subsequent action you have taken. In fact this becomes a legal obligation if your company has five or more employees. Such records may well help to demonstrate that you have taken all reasonable care to ensure that safety standards have been properly considered and acted upon. They might also play a key role in any enquiry or proceedings should an accident occur.

Step 5 Review and revise

Perhaps this is not an obvious step, but in fact it is a vital one. This step recognises that situations change, and that from a safety point of view, measures put in place to *avoid* and *reduce* hazard and risk need to be kept under constant review. At its most blindingly obvious, a perfectly safe location for your shoot might easily become fraught with danger after rain. Such dangers would include the possibility of slipping or of electric shock if lighting or cables were in use. This particular example should of course never arise, because experience and imagination would suggest that this eventuality would be considered from the outset. A more realistic situation would be one where for various reasons members of the public are unexpectedly found in far greater numbers in close vicinity to a shoot, or for instance when a quiet road becomes unexpectedly busy because of a last-minute diversion. Having reviewed the original assessment, you should, of course, be ready to make whatever adjustments are required because of the changes which have taken place. Revisiting the assessment may well also alert you to hazards you had not previously recognised.

These then are the most basic steps, the building blocks on which you can build your own Health and Safety policy should you be working in a situation where such a policy is not provided for you.

Developing a system

Having a policy is one thing, but in order to implement and maintain it, certain systems need to be developed to facilitate continuing and systematic compliance, not only with your own policy, but with the requirements of the law. The detail of such systems will naturally vary widely according to the needs and circumstances of the production unit in question. There are, however, a number of clear principles which should underlie the development of such a system:

1   **Legal obligations**: Any system introduced must at the very least ensure that compliance with legal obligations is observed. It follows therefore that you should be aware of what these legal duties and obligations are. Trade organisations such as PACT (www.pact.co.uk) will be able to advise on the details as will the HSE. For less formally constituted or *ad hoc* bodies, such as student production groups or community associations, then the relevant authorities should be consulted and will invariably have a policy of compliance in place. Should this not be the case, then the development of such a policy or system should be requested at the earliest

opportunity. Common sense suggests that any group, whether or not it legally constitutes a company or undertakes the role of employer, would be well advised to act at all times as if it were subject to such obligations. In other words, a cautious and careful approach to compliance is to be recommended.

2   **Responsibility**: It is very important that the entire production team or organisation is aware of the responsibility for Health and Safety and where such responsibility lies. This may, for example, be on a legal basis involving the duty of care by the commissioner or client. Indeed no broadcaster will commission without being sure that the production company concerned has the appropriate expertise and training in Health and Safety. There is also the need for complete clarity in terms of the day-to-day responsibility for the implementation of Health and Safety policy and systems within the production team or crew. This task will often, of course, be undertaken by the Production Manager, but in a small organisation where no one is formally undertaking a PM role, the situation might be less clear. In such circumstances it is doubly important that key responsibilities are unmistakably allocated and that each member of the team is aware of them. Finally it is worth pointing out that despite the requirement for the clear allocation of responsibility (and authority) for Health and Safety, every member of the team needs to feel that they play an important part in ensuring the safety of everyone on that team, working with it or near it.

3   **Control**: While it is obviously important to clarify responsibility for Health and Safety, clarity is also essential when it comes to exercising control over various members of the crew or team, or indeed of the location or premises which are being used. It is difficult to implement safety procedures effectively if it is not clear where such control lies. Grey areas give rise to ambiguity and in matters of Health and Safety this is to be avoided at all costs. Important questions of control can arise if contractors are employed in the course of a production and it needs to be established at the outset where responsibility and authority lie. An example of where this could be important is when shooting in an outdoor location with lights. At what point should shooting be halted or suspended when it starts to rain? In my own experience of such a situation, the complications were compounded by the fact that the shoot took place at night, children were involved and the location was a scrap

yard and full of physical hazards. In such circumstances it is not always clear where control should lie, with the director (who naturally wants to get the shots in the can), the camera operator who has similar motivations or the sparks (electrician) who might want, sensibly, to 'pull the plug'! It is easy to assert in this case that we should listen to the electrician. If, however, the sparks declares himself happy to carry on despite the cables, the rain and the puddles, who then should decide to stop work? Here the situation becomes less clear yet more critical. Restricted budgets and tight schedules will always provide an incentive to push ahead; Health and Safety requires caution and careful consideration.

4   **Integration:** In its guidance to production companies, the Health and Safety Executive (HSE) underlines how important it is that Health and Safety is fully integrated with all the activities undertaken by the production unit (HSE (2006) *INDG360 Health and Safety in audiovisual production, your legal duties* [Internet]. Available: www/hse.gov.uk/pubns/indg360.pdf [accessed 1 July 2008]). In other words, Health and Safety should take its place alongside editorial and dramatic decision-making and be fully integrated with the planning and organisation of productions. Systems set up to ensure best practice and safe working conditions should not be seen as a bolt-on extra, or even worse as a last minute irksome requirement. An example of the kind of integration to be achieved would be to ensure that a formal part of each 'recce' includes undertaking a risk assessment of the site. In this way Health and Safety systems (the risk assessment) are tightly integrated with the creative and editorial assessment and subsequent scheduling of the shoot.

5   **Communication:** However good the risk assessments, their effectiveness will inevitably be weakened if the identification of risks and the steps to be taken to eliminate or reduce them are not widely and openly available to everyone involved. This is again largely down to attitude. If Health and Safety is seen to be important then awareness is increased throughout the production unit or company. If, on the other hand, risk assessments and other systems are seen merely as irritating and ancillary tasks then the danger is that forms will be filed away unread by those who most need to be aware of the identification of possible hazards.

6   **Monitoring:** For any system to be efficient and effective, its practice requires to be monitored on a regular and systematic basis. There are a number of obvious reasons for this. Monitoring will help to ensure that the requirements of the system are being observed across the production team and not ignored and neglected by some. Such monitoring will also ensure that if systems need to be modified, the need to do so will quickly become apparent and such modifications can be made. An example of this might be utterly basic – there is not enough room on the form supplied adequately to account for measures to control risks which have been identified. The simple remedy is to modify the form as soon as possible, otherwise the exercise will be neglected or taken less seriously than it ought to be. A further example of the benefits of monitoring might be that it could become clear that for the system to work well, the risk assessment form needs to be 'signed off' by a senior member of the team and not simply filed away as soon as it is completed. In this way, those ultimately responsible for the safety of the team and those associated with it can be sure that Health and Safety issues are being taken as seriously as possible.

The risk assessment

Of all the paperwork involved in Health and Safety, the key document is the risk assessment form. The five basic steps to risk assessment (outlined above) make a fairly major contribution to the layout of the forms required for the job. We need to be clear at the outset that the example we are working on here is for a relatively simple location shoot with a small crew. More complicated set-ups will inevitably require more detailed information and check-lists. Working with vehicles, firearms and pyrotechnics are simply examples of many situations where specialist training, experience and risk assessment procedures are essential.

Again the Health and Safety Executive has a number of publications available that are targeted at specialist situations, which are likely to be encountered in the audiovisual industries, and most of these can be downloaded as PDFs. Full details are given in the reference section at the end of this book. Also listed are the contact details for agencies and organisations, such as PACT and Skillset, which offer specialised training in Health and Safety at various levels. The importance of professional

Risk assessment form			
Company or production name		Date of risk assessment	
Identify the hazards	Who might be harmed?	Evaluate the risks	Action required
1	2	3	4
Review of assessment: *Record any changes and measures required, if neccessary amend the risk assessment.*			
Date Reviewed:			
Carried out by:			

Figure 6.1 A simple risk assessment form

training and experience cannot be emphasised enough and it is well worth enquiring about discounts and grants to help you to access this training.

The risk assessment form needs to be as simple as possible, yet at the same time allowing for relevant and important detail to be entered. At a basic level, the HSA leaflet *'Five steps to risk assessment'* (Health and Safety Executive (2006) *INDG163(rev2) Five steps to risk assessment* [Internet]. Available www.hse.gov.uk/pubns/indg163.pdf [accessed 1 July 2008]) not only provides an easy-to-read explanation of the procedure but thoughtfully provides a simple one-page risk assessment form at the end (Health and Safety Executive (2006) *Risk assessment template* [Internet]. Available: www.hse.gov.uk/risk/template.pdf [accessed 1 July 2008]). This form is also available as a template. Both documents are freely available to download and can with very few restrictions be freely used and reproduced in connection with your work.

7
Managing rights/ compliance

Introduction

In this chapter, we look first at some of the general issues surrounding the whole subject of compliance and the reasons it is so important to get it right. Then we will take a closer look at each area of compliance with some suggestions as to how you might ensure that as a production unit, you comply with all your responsibilities and that you keep accurate paperwork. This will not only help you to achieve compliance but will also prove that you have done so. Experienced Production Managers will have ready access to forms and templates, guidance notes and professional advice when it comes to compliance issues. This chapter is intended as a helpful introduction to those who do not have such access but for whom compliance is still a very necessary part of production management. It will look at the range of compliance matters from employing actors and writers, to making sure that any music you use is both logged accurately and cleared with the appropriate authority. Wherever possible, you will be referred to agencies and organisations where you can obtain more detailed information and advice when you need it. Some suggestions will also be made as to how you can design your own forms, adapt mine or download others to enable you to manage your compliance easily and efficiently. Health and Safety is, of course, a compliance issue, but is so important that it has been dealt with separately in the previous chapter.

I have heard recently of one production company which has had to cease trading, largely because it failed to ensure that it kept proper records of copyright material it used and did not obtain the necessary licences to use such material in advance. It stands to reason that if you have used an extract of copyright material such as music or video in your programme and have not negotiated a licence *in advance* then your negotiating position later on is very much weakened, especially if the material in question plays a vital part in the finished programme. Even worse is to succumb to the temptation to bury your head and to proceed to complete the programme without the required clearances in the hope that no one notices. The chances are that they will! Digital technology and the ability to find a great deal of material on the Internet has made it very easy to obtain a great deal of illustrative material. The problem is that the vast bulk of it is copyright and belongs to someone else. Unauthorised use can lead to catastrophic consequences and the intervention of the law and lawyers and is to be avoided at all costs. This advice applies equally to student productions, amateurs, community groups and independent film production regardless of end use, whether the final programme is to be broadcast, streamed on the Internet or entered into competition. Limited budgets place huge pressures on producers, and those responsible for production management need to be vigilant in order to safeguard the integrity of the completed product. Individuals and even corporations can be very generous in allowing impoverished programme-makers access to material they own, but to do so they have to be asked – it is always worth a try!

Compliance is a general term which refers to the duty of a production unit to ensure that it *complies* with the law, with regulations and with agreements to which it is subject or which are relevant to it. Three examples might help to clarify and sharpen this definition:

1   **The law**: Those producing a programme must ensure that nothing that is said or done in the programme or in the making of the programme falls foul of the law. Such matters might include racial abuse, indecency or any other activity which the law condemns. Such laws, of course, apply to everyone, broadcasters included, and cover a wide range of issues. Broadcasters such as the BBC and Channel 4 will require completion of their own designated paperwork closely detailing every area of compliance, and to some degree this makes it easier for a production company to ensure that they stay on the right side of the law and governance. Advice and guidance is readily available from compliance officers within the broadcasting organisations. It may well be one of the roles of the Production Manager to be alert and sensitive to issues which require referral to senior members of the team or, of course, for legal advice. In a small production team, where production management is a shared responsibility, serious consideration should be given to the advisability of a single person within the team taking responsibility for compliance.

2   **Regulation**: Your activity, if it involves broadcasting, will be governed by OFCOM (Office of Communications, www.ofcom. org.uk), which has put in place a number of regulations which cover a variety of issues such as impartiality, offensive material, the right to privacy and the protection of young people.

3   **Agreements**: You may well have made arrangements with a third party to use clips from other programmes or films. If this is the case, then it is essential that the content of such agreements is observed.

Other agreements may also be in force whether or not you are directly a party to them. For instance, PACT (Producers' Alliance for Cinema and Television) has agreements with Equity (the actors' union) on agreed rates of pay for actors in various types of activity, from broadcast drama to appearances in corporate productions and voice-over work. These agreements have been negotiated on behalf of PACT members who are bound by them.

The lines of demarcation between legal requirements, regulations and agreements are inevitably blurred. For example, *regulations* made by OFCOM will be binding on an organisation because of powers granted in the Communications Act 2003. So regulations may have the force of law and, of course, any *agreements* you make may be enforced by the law.

Again, it should be emphasised that this book makes no claim to legal expertise of any kind, but rather it aims to alert you to issues of compliance which are crucial in the smooth running of programme production and of production companies.

In order to clarify issues of compliance and where they are likely to occur, we will look first at people taking part in your programme and the agreements you may need to cover their participation. Then we will go on to tackle the issue of copyright and how it may affect material you might wish to include. Finally, in this chapter, we will outline some of the paperwork which could help you at a fairly elementary level to keep track of compliance issues.

Although not strictly necessary, it is probably advisable to ensure that for every participant in your programme there is a corresponding paper agreement in your files. This agreement ensures your right to use the material that has been recorded for the programme (and quite often for any other purpose you choose). The precise content of such agreements will depend on the nature of the programme being made, the nature of the contribution to be made and the professional status of your contributor.

Working with actors

The use of members of the acting profession is subject to a number of agreements between the actors' union, Equity (www.equity.org.uk) and a number of organisations. According to its web site:

Equity is the only Trade Union to represent artists from across the entire spectrum of arts and entertainment. Formed in 1930 by a group of West End of London performers, Equity quickly spread to encompass the whole range of professional entertainment so our membership includes actors, singers, dancers, choreographers, stage managers, theatre directors and designers, variety and circus artists, television and radio presenters, walk-on and supporting artists, stunt performers and directors and theatre fight directors. (www.equity.org.uk/AboutUs/WhatIsEquity.aspx [accessed 31 August 2008])

This suggests that many, if not most, of those professionals you may wish to contribute to your production team's programme will be covered by Equity agreements. It is important to understand that this applies not simply to drama productions but to factual programmes too. So, for instance, a presenter recording a narration for a short documentary might well be an Equity member and expect at least the minimum Equity rate for the job. You may be undertaking the production management for a student group or for a small production company, neither of which will presumably have directly negotiated an agreement with Equity nor be a member of an organisation which has negotiated such an agreement on behalf of its members. Nevertheless, any Equity member will expect that any agreement he or she makes with you will be made in accordance with the relevant Equity agreement. This will cover not only the fee, but other items such as expenses, meals allowances and rest breaks. In addition, these agreements will usually specify and restrict the right to use the recorded performance to particular territories (for example, Europe) and to the number of transmissions (in the case of broadcast) before a repeat fee is payable. Repeat fees are usually expressed as a percentage of the original fee. Remember too that extras (more properly referred to as walk-on artists) are also covered by Equity agreements, and will expect a certain minimum rate of pay depending on what exactly they are expected to do. PACT members will have access to a variety of contract templates as well as advice on various issues which may arise when engaging Equity members. Student groups, independent film-makers and small start-up companies may well not have ready access to such advice. In this case you should consider setting up your own letter template which covers the essential points of any agreement. Again, it should be clear that you should always seek advice if you have any anxiety about the terms of any agreement or contract that you make in the course of your production.

Working with the public

In this context, the public refers to those people who are not engaged by you as 'talent'. Such participants, usually actors, are dealt with in the sections above. Simply put, this section is likely to be more relevant to those making factual and documentary productions. It therefore includes all your interviewees and members of the public that in some way *feature* in your programme. The idea of identifying those who feature in the programme helps you to make commonsense decisions when you need to decide who needs to sign a release form enabling you to use the material you have recorded with them. This commonsense approach would mean, for example, that if you conduct a vox pop with a member of the public, you should ask them to sign a release. You would not need to ask passers-by who happen to walk through the frame to fill in a form. Other circumstances may be less clear. If you are filming in an identifiable location you need to be sensitive to the fact that some members of the public might not want to be seen there for perfectly legitimate and private reasons. An example of this might be outside a doctor's surgery when members of the public entering or leaving might be easily identified when the clip is broadcast. The same might be true in a shop or any other particular and clearly defined place. In these circumstances it can often help to put up a warning notice in advance, announcing the forthcoming shoot. You would, of course, have to use discretion in such circumstances where, for example, such advance warning might attract individuals intent on distracting behaviour or disrupting the shoot completely.

It is also worth giving careful consideration to the situation when filming abroad. You cannot assume that laws, customs and practices are the same in all countries, and if you have any doubts you should consult those with experience or expertise on foreign filming assignments. The public in the UK is far more relaxed about appearing incidentally in a shot. In the US for instance, there appears to be more sensitivity and even hostility in such circumstances. It goes without saying that cultural differences can be very important, so that filming women may cause great offence in some Muslim and other societies, for example.

As far as I understand the situation, there is no legal reason for a release to be signed before material is edited and broadcast. The requirement has been imposed for understandable reasons by various broadcasters and other organisations as a kind of 'belt-and braces' approach so that there is a piece of paper in existence to 'prove' that an individual has actively consented to the use of their contribution. I would therefore strongly advise the use of such consent forms in all circumstances and wherever possible, though the absence of such a signed form does not necessarily prevent its use and broadcast. You may well find, however, that a broadcaster would not accept such a situation. I recall one incident a number of years ago when my own production team interviewed a member of what was then known as the Board of Governors of the BBC. The interview had been arranged in advance and took place in the interviewee's own home. The interviewer was a well-known broadcaster and a personal friend of the interviewee. The interview went well, but the interviewee refused to sign a release form on the grounds that she had obviously consented to be interviewed and did not intend to sign a piece of paper granting rights 'throughout the Universe' although she readily consented to such use. I had a great deal of sympathy with her position, and did not try to insist in a signature. The interview was of course edited into the programme and subsequently broadcast by the BBC to everyone's satisfaction. This anecdote does not, however, detract from the position that wherever possible, such consent forms need to be signed to keep commissioners happy and sheltered from possible litigation, however unlikely! One helpful tip is that where you do not have access to a clearance form on location, you can ask the participant to confirm their consent to your use of the material while *on camera*; in this way you do at least have tangible evidence should you need it later.

The programme budget will have specified whether or not an allowance has been made to pay contributors for their appearance in the programme. No payment needs to change hands in order for the contributor to sign a release form although if payment is made, then the amended form (Figure 7.2) is the ideal place to record this *consideration* or fee.

The consent form or release (sometimes called a *blood chit*) needs to contain details of the company or production unit responsible for the programme, the title of the production, the date of the shoot and the name and if possible the address of the contributor. An example of a simple release form is given (Figure 7.1) and is also available to download from this book's web site. In all cases, there should be two copies of the release form, one to be retained by the production, the other to be given to the contributor.

```
                    HYPOTHETICAL PRODUCTIONS LTD
                     21 Tripod Street Bristol XXX XXX
                          Tel. 1234 5678

Production/programme name _____


 Name of Contributor          Nature of contribution (please specify)
 Address 1
 Address 2
 Address 3
 Postcode
  Date:


In consideration of the above production company agreeing that I contribute to and participate in the above programme, the
nature of which has been fully explained to me, I hereby consent to the use of my contribution in the above programme. I agree
that the copyright of this contribution shall be wholly vested in the company .

I agree to any future exploitation of this contribution by the company in all media and formats through out the universe.




 Signed by the Contributor: _____


 Name (Please print) _____ Date:_____


 Signed by: _____


 On behalf of: _____ Production Company Date:_____
```

Figure 7.1 Simple release form (no fee)

Working with writers

You should be aware that in many areas of creative work, agreements have already been negotiated between broadcasters, independent producers and writers. It is therefore quite possible that any arrangement you wish to make with a writer for a drama script or commentary will be subject to the conditions and minimum payments negotiated as part of this agreement with the Writers' Guild of Great Britain (www. writersguild.org.uk). According to this organisation:

> The Writers' Guild of Great Britain is the trade union representing writers in TV, radio, theatre, books, poetry, film

---

HYPOTHETICAL PRODUCTIONS LTD
21 Tripod Street Bristol XXX XXX
Tel. 1234 5678

Production/programme name_____

I acknowledge receipt of the sum of £_____ in consideration of my contribution to and
participation in the above programme, the nature of which has been fully explained to me, I hereby consent
to the use of my contribution in the above programme. I agree that the copyright of this contribution shall
be wholly vested in the company .

I agree to any future exploitation of this contribution by the company in all media and formats through
out the universe.

Signed by the Contributor: _____

Name (Please print) _____ Date:_____

Signed by:_____

On behalf of: _____ Production Company Date:_____

Figure 7.2 Simple release form (for fee)

and video games. In TV, film, radio and theatre, the Guild is
the recognised body for negotiating for writers.

The Writers' Guild is possibly less familiar to producers than Equity.
Most producers and Production Managers will have worked with actors
at one time or another; it is perhaps less likely that they have
commissioned writers. It is also true to say that some of those who do
write for television may not be members of the Writers' Guild. This
is more likely to be the case in factual television. In drama genres it is
almost certain that you will be dealing with a member of the Guild. In
either case, it is advisable to assume that you need to observe the terms
and conditions of the various agreements that the Guild has negotiated
with different sectors of the industry. The full range of these agreements

is easily accessible on the Guild's web site. It is certainly advisable for those responsible for production management to be reasonably familiar with the television agreement. This not only outlines the minimum agreed rates, but also covers many contingencies which might arise during a production and in the course of your relationship with a writer. Perusing an agreement which runs to just under 30 pages of typescript might seem a little onerous yet it provides a helpful check-list of the issues of which you should be aware. These cover everyday matters such as basic fees and subsistence allowances if you need the writer on location or on set but also what is to happen in the case of re-writes and disputes. It also stipulates the rights and responsibilities of both sides as well as the allocation of residual payments if, for example, the programme is sold abroad or sold as a published DVD.

Working with music, composers and musicians

This can be a difficult and complex area and you may be well advised to seek assistance if you have any doubts or uncertainties. It may be helpful, however, to break down your use of music into three principal areas:

- The composer (of words and/or music)
- The musicians or performers
- The actual recording.

Your compliance and clearance needs to cover all three of these areas if you have commissioned music for your programme. If, however, you have only made use of recorded music, then your concern will be with three areas of compliance:

- Sync rights (in order to be able to put music you have recorded onto your edited picture)
- Dubbing rights (similar to sync rights but applicable when you are using pre-recorded music – usually from CD
- Broadcast rights (in order to be able to show the programme in one or more territory).

You therefore need to consider which rights you need to clear, and to ensure that you do so with the correct body. This might well be a 'collecting organisation', which does exactly what the name suggests. Collecting organisations represent their members and undertake to collect fees due to them for the use of their work.

It is perfectly possible, even on a modest programme, that you will wish to engage the services of musicians to write and to perform on the soundtrack. In terms of composers, the question of agreements and compliance are a little less straightforward than in other areas you might have to deal with. This is because unlike actors and writers, there is no single body which represents the interests of composers and songwriters. Consequently there are no standard minimum agreements and sample contracts are therefore more difficult to access. As in most areas however, PACT members do have access to sample contracts and to guidance as to how these should be completed and operated. Smaller production units will need to construct their own agreements with composers they commission to write music for a programme. Even if friends are writing (and possibly recording) music, a written agreement is advisable and may be a necessity. Many competitions and festivals will, for example, refuse to screen a programme if all compliance issues have not been covered by written agreements, and will require undertakings from the producers that such agreements are in existence. If you draw up your own contract or agreement with a composer you will need to consider a range of questions. These will include arrangements, orchestrations and possible performance of the music, whether the composed music remains the intellectual property of the composer or whether you as the producer buy these rights and if such rights are limited to particular use (for example, terrestrial television) in specified territories (for example, Europe). It is an interesting aside to note that in most media agreements 'the world' no longer exists and 'worldwide rights' are more likely to be defined as 'throughout the universe'!

As far as *performance* is concerned, the situation is much clearer. Musicians in the UK are represented by the Musicians' Union (www.musiciansunion. org.uk), often known as the MU. According to this organisation:

> The Musicians' Union represents over thirty thousand musicians working in all sectors of the music business.

> As well as negotiating on behalf of our members with all the major employers in the industry, we offer a range of services for professional and student musicians of all ages.

Many arrangers as well as musicians are represented by the MU and are parties to agreements between the union and producers (through PACT) and broadcasters such as the BBC and C4. If you are considering using the services of musicians in your production, then your best course of action is to talk to your local branch as soon as possible. As with all kinds of contributors, it is in the interests of all parties that agreements should be made at the outset. There is no surer way of blowing a hole in your budget (or destroying it completely) than by having to negotiate fees and rights retrospectively when you are in the weakest position and therefore unable to bargain effectively.

Most commonly however, producers make use of music which has already been recorded. Such recorded music will usually fall into one of two categories, commercial music or library music.

Commercial music is music (popular or classical) which is published and available to buy from a store or online. You do not have any automatic right to use such music and each use of it must be negotiated (in advance) with copyright owners, that is composers, musicians and the owners of the actual recording (usually a record label). Each of these owners will have to give permission and agree a fee. It will already be clear that you are therefore embarking on what could well turn out to be a complicated and protracted process. If you have been commissioned by a major broadcaster such as the BBC, then you may benefit from what is known as the 'blanket agreement' whereby the BBC pays a very large fee on an annual basis to cover music copyright payments for commercial recordings in its broadcasts. If you are in this happy situation then, of course, the broadcaster will advise what procedures you will need to undertake. In all other circumstances, you will need to take steps in advance in order to agree the clearance of the music you want to use.

Library music, which may also be described as royalty-free music or production music, is music which is specially recorded for use in the audiovisual industries. This kind of music is sometimes erroneously referred to as 'copyright free', but this is certainly not the case. In effect the owners of the music and the recordings agree to make it available to productions without prior clearance as long as such use is duly logged, reported and paid for. This makes for a simple system where costs can be calculated accurately in advance. In exchange for a reporting log and the appropriate fee, a licence will be issued making clear the territories for which the licence is issued, and the purposes for which it has been issued, for example, for a broadcast programme, a commercial or an audio-visual presentation. Details of clearance and costs for most production music libraries can be obtained from the MCPS-PRS Alliance (MCPS-PRS Alliance [an alliance of the Mechanical Copyright Protection Society and the Performing Rights Society], an important collection agency for music clearance for the audiovisual industries; www.mcps.prs.alliance.co.uk). This is a non-profit organisation representing musicians, composers and copyright owners in a kind of one-stop-shop for those who wish to use music in their productions. Whatever your requirements for recorded music (including much commercial music), the Alliance will be able to offer helpful advice and a visit to explore its web site is greatly recommended and will enable you better to understand the steps you need to undertake in order to accurately report and obtain clearance for your music use. In a relatively new innovation (2007), independent production companies can now apply to the Alliance for a blanket agreement for the use of music in programmes for a variety of broadcast uses at fixed fees depending, as usual, on territory and delivery method.

Whatever decisions you reach on the music to be used in your production, you will need to keep accurate records of such usage, and this is usually done on a music reporting form. Some organisations will supply their own forms, or in the case of the MCPS-PRS Alliance, allow you to do so online. There is, however, no substitute for your own music logging form and a sample form is shown in Figure 7.3 and provided for your use on the website associated with this book.

Company/production unit name
MUSIC REPORTING FORM (CUE SHEET)

Disc name	Disc No.	Track name	Track No.	Composer	Publisher	Duration Mins	Secs	Notes

Production title:
Date:
Completed by:

Figure 7.3 Basic music reporting form

You should use your own music reporting form to note music tracks *as they are used*. In this way you will make sure that details are not lost, even if the disc you used does go astray. Even if you use one section of music repeatedly you should note that most music libraries and publishers require each use to be reported separately and not aggregated. If you use your form during the edit and any subsequent dubbing session you will be able to use the data you have collected to make your official return quickly and efficiently. The form above will suffice for most simple logging of music information. There will, however, be occasions where a more sophisticated and detailed record is required. The form in Figure 7.4 provides for a rather more detailed record, but like the simpler form,

Company/production unit name
MUSIC REPORTING FORM (CUE SHEET)

Production title: _____
Date: _____
Completed by: _____

Disc name	Disc no.	Track no.	Disc label		
Composer		Performer	Arranger		Publisher
Duration used	Min	Secs	Notes		

Disc name	Disc no.	Track no.	Disc label		
Composer		Performer	Arranger		Publisher
Duration used	Min	Secs	Notes		

Disc name	Disc no.	Track no	Disc label		
Composer		Performer	Arranger		Publisher
Duration used	Min	Secs	Notes		

Disc name	Disc no.	Track no.	Disc label		

Figure 7.4 A more detailed music reporting form

may be easily adapted for your own particular needs. Both forms are available to download from the web site associated with this book.

On the second form you will be able to input a rather more detailed account of the music you have selected. In this form, each page provides room for five entries and can include notes. In the notes section, for example, you may wish to include details of the time-code in and out points to pin-point exactly where the music begins and ends in the production. Both the forms provided can be easily adapted to your own particular requirements.

Working with children and young people

This section is not intended as a statement of the law on working with children or young people, but rather as an alert to those responsible for production management in these circumstances. You should be aware that the law concerning the use of children in drama or any other context is both rigorous and fairly complex; for example, the Children and Young Persons Act (1933) and subsequent legislation and the Children (Performances) Regulation (1968). The enforcement of these regulations is generally part of the remit of the relevant local authority, which generally takes such matters very seriously. In most circumstances a licence will be required, and other regulations stipulate the presence of chaperones and the provision, for example, of separate changing and toilet facilities. Those without the relevant experience or training in these issues will be well advised to seek expert help if they intend to work with children who are below the minimum school-leaving age.

In addition, you should be aware that in any situation where you are working in proximity to children you need to take special care to ensure that individual children are not identified without their parents' informed consent. Perfectly legitimate filming at or near a school may require such parental consent (usually in writing) if the children are in shot (even if unintentionally). Such restrictions should be observed even in cases when the editorial content of your programme is completely uncontentious. Children involved in legal proceedings of any kind are subject to a further raft of protection. It should be stressed that if your production requires the participation of children, whether paid or unpaid, you should investigate the situation very carefully and in plenty of time. If, for example, a licence is required, it can take a matter of weeks to acquire.

Working with archives and other material

It is safe to assume that copyright will exist in any material you wish to insert into your programme. Such material may consist of inserts from other programmes, old archive film or recordings, sound and pictures of any kind. Wherever possible you should try to work through established libraries that have the expertise in the licensing of the material which they control. The reference section of this book contains information on a selection of libraries which can supply archive material for inclusion in audiovisual productions.

I strongly suggest that directors and editors are provided with a form similar to that in Figure 7.5, so that a record can be kept of any third-party material as it is edited into the programme. This should help you to ensure that you do not miss a vital sequence and that the Production Manager can ensure that proper clearances have been obtained. The first column records a description of the subject matter, while column 2 is concerned with as accurate a description of the source as possible. The other columns are fairly self-explanatory, and the time-code entry and exit points are used so that the precise point at which the material is inserted into the final programme can be quickly identified. The document heading reminds the user that this form is not suitable for music reporting because music logs require specific and precise information.

Copyright is a complex legal field, and copyright owners will often rigorously pursue those who they feel have breached their rights and used their material without the relevant clearances. Copyright is protected

Copyright material log (not for music reporting)					
Company or production name: _____ Date:_____					
Brief description of material	Details of source	Format	T/c in	T/c out	Notes
Time lapse seed sprouts	DvD Stirling Films	DVD	01:17:26	01:28:13	Pre-cleared

Figure 7.5 Copyright logging form

by both criminal and civil law, and the penalties for breaches can be severe. Again, it would be wise to construct a form in order to record the use of archive material from third parties in your programme. The form can then be used both in pre-production as agreements are negotiated (as far in advance as possible!) throughout the production period, and most importantly as clips are edited into the final programme in post-production. Use of archive material is usually charged by the second on its use in the final programme (along with ancillary search fees and dubbing charges where these are specified) so it is once again of the utmost important to keep an accurate record of both sources and timings. The outline form in Figure 7.5 should be of help in maintaining records, and the online version can be easily adapted to your own requirements.

Part III
Production management in action

In the previous chapters of this book we have looked at the qualities needed by the Production Manager in order to see a production successfully and efficiently to its conclusion. We have analysed the principal areas of responsibility such as scheduling and Health and Safety and examined ways in which to track and record the work which has been done. This third section, 'Production management in action' is an attempt to organise these tasks and responsibilities into an expanded check-list for you to adapt and use as you plan, carry out and finalise your programmes. In other words, we are going to look at production management as it impinges on the three key phases of programme making, pre-production, production and post-production. Again, it is important to bear in mind that this is not a rigid, one-way process. No programmes, even tightly formatted ones, can be successfully managed according to an inflexible set of rules and timetables. These rules, forms and schedules will need to be constantly adjusted in order to cope with the exigencies of working in the real world. This is perhaps the essential mark of good production management; to construct a solid management framework which enables an excellent programme to be made with the minimum of stress and a maximum of efficiency, while at the same time being flexible enough to respond to the needs of the programme and of the team making it.

I suppose that good Production Managers achieve this blend of system and flexibility almost instinctively, and continue to develop it as their professional lives provide them with increasing experience and expertise. For the relatively inexperienced, it is a good goal to focus on. In my experience as a producer and as a production teacher, I have noticed that contrary to popular myth, outstanding programmes rarely emerge from chaotic production units. Most often the reverse is true and that the best and most creative efforts are usually the result certainly of vision, but vision which flourishes in a setting which provides clearly defined and efficient working practices. Perhaps the whole notion of production management and certainly excellent production management is a daily endorsement of the maxim attributed to Thomas Edison that 'genius is one per cent inspiration and ninety-nine per cent perspiration'!

What follows is a step-by-step guide through the entire production process. These guides are principally targeted at production management for small programme-making teams such as student groups or new independent production companies. The assumption therefore will be that all tasks need to be accounted for within the remit of production management, while at the same time acknowledging that not all these tasks will actually fall to the Production Manager in the real world of broadcast or large-scale corporate production. The important point to bear in mind is that if the production is to be managed successfully and efficiently, all these individual tasks must be completed; *this* is production management, whoever is doing it!

8
Pre-production

Producers and crews are usually (and understandably) extremely anxious to start the practical work of filming. The check-list below, which makes no attempt to be exhaustive, indicates just how much has to be achieved in terms of production management before an inch of tape or a frame of film has been shot. Purists in the business would, of course, be quick to point out that the section I have described as 'development' would not usually be regarded as an integral part of pre-production and certainly not generally part of the work of the Production Manager. While this is true, it seemed to me that in a book aimed primarily at those still at an early stage in their experience of working in television production, it was well worthwhile including some of these preliminaries in the check-list.

The check-list in Figure 8.1 is available from the web site associated with this book as two separate files, one for factual programmes and the other for drama/feature productions.

Development

Research: a frequent mistake of the inexperienced is to underestimate the amount of time, skill, patience and sheer bloody-mindedness that is required before a project even gets to the pre-production stage. This tendency is possibly more significant in areas of factual programming such as documentaries. After all, it is pretty obvious that you cannot start a feature film or drama without developing a script. While it is highly unlikely that you would ever want to develop a script for a documentary, the ideas and focus certainly need to be developed and refined. Production management often involves asking tough questions and this early stage is certainly one of the times when such questions

Pre-production check-list		
Factual		**Feature/drama**
Development		
Research		
Outline		
Proposal/brief/pitch		
Budget agreement		
Pre-production		
Buget breakdown*		
Insurance		
Purchase orders*		
Equipment booked		
Crewing		
Recce/location finding		
Risk assessments*		
Shot list*		
Schedules*		
Call sheets*		
Contact sheet*		
Licensing/clearances*		
Shot logging*		
* Indicates that an associated form is available on-line		

Figure 8.1 Pre-production check-list

are entirely appropriate. Is it possible to express the story the programme is going to tell succinctly and in a sentence or two? If not then it is more than likely that the idea needs more work, more focus and some sharper ideas. Most factual productions made by less experienced programme-makers are woefully under-researched. It is true that research should always continue throughout a production, but this means that the producer or director should always be alert to new developments in their subject matter; it should not mean that the basics of finding interviewees and locations should still be taking place when shooting has started. Flexibility is a virtue; lack of preparation (that is, research) can be fatal in terms of the quality and coherence of the final programme.

The outline is a desirable document for the Production Manager to have to hand as it should provide a clear statement of what the programme is about, a kind of précis of the subject matter or the format of a factual programme. Such an outline might be extremely helpful when negotiating the use of facilities or locations and will help those responsible for production management to explain what the programme is about to those whose cooperation is sought. The very act of explaining a programme briefly and succinctly can help everyone in the team, and as they say, 'it sharpens the mind'!

The proposal, brief and pitch are not essentially part of pre-production yet they play a crucial role in the development and presentation of a programme idea, and again, someone has to do it. In a large production company this may well be done at executive producer level. In a smaller unit this remit may well form part of the portfolio of jobs undertaken by the Production Manager or by those who share the work of production management. This is not the place to enlarge on the possibilities and pitfalls of pitching or writing proposals and treatments and such help can be found from a variety of sources. I would, however, want to stress the importance of this stage in the development of ideas for television; the discipline required of putting an attractive proposition onto a couple of sides of paper is well worth the effort it takes and will without doubt raise helpful questions in the minds of the producers well before these become awkward questions in the minds of clients, commissioners or funders.

The budget agreement is the final and essential step before the work of pre-production can begin. This is the agreed global figure, the bottom line for production costs. Many commissioners provide guide prices for productions; such a price will provide the figure you need for the budget agreement stage and will enable you to go forward to break down costs into a detailed budget (see Chapter 4). Your budget may, of course, be zero, you may be working for expenses only or as part of a student production where facilities are provided as part of a course. You should not let this situation of what we might describe as a zero budget suggest that budgeting is unnecessary. Equipment and time are resources just as much as cash, and it will be to your advantage to work out what the use of camera and recording equipment, for example, would cost if you had to pay for them. In this way you would be able to construct a budget breakdown (see below). This is a useful, eye-opening and constructive exercise and provides invaluable experience for future use.

Script development for feature drama projects will have been the major preoccupation of the development phase in this genre and you should ensure that this work, along with the budget agreement, has been completed before proceeding to pre-production.

Pre-production

Budget breakdown is one of the major tasks for production management, at this stage to produce a budget breakdown, or if this has already been provided, to check the budget both in terms of the allocation of funds to cost centres and to ensure that no significant item has been omitted. These tasks should be carried out as soon as possible and certainly before bookings are made for crew, cast and equipment; in other words check your budgets before you commit yourself to spending money!

Purchase orders are an essential way of controlling and tracking your budgets. A purchase order (usually numbered) signed by the Production Manager or other designated person should be the only authorised way of spending production budgets other than on crewing and wages. The introduction of such a system is to be highly recommended. Consequently it is vital that every member of the production team is aware that the system is in place and how it is to be operated. This means also that there will need to be a clear understanding of the monetary limits of petty cash purchases and what these are. Financial controls are easily breached if relatively expensive items such as car hire or travel tickets are purchased in this way and to do so inevitably means that regular financial reporting becomes infinitely more complicated. Suppliers also need to know that you are operating a purchase order system and that they should not supply goods or services without first obtaining a purchase order or at least a purchase order number from an authorised person.

Insurance is included in your check-list as a reminder that if your production requires any kind of cover such as completion insurance or special cover for hazardous situations, then forms actually need to be completed and submitted as soon as possible! For the small start-up production company, this may also be a good point at which to remind you of the absolute necessity of obtaining public liability insurance in case your work results in an accident for which you could be found liable.

Scripting work constitutes a large proportion of the work of production management in the pre-production of features. Shooting cannot take place until a shooting script has been prepared and a script breakdown carried out in parallel with the budget breakdown and casting (Chapter 5).

You might wish to place preliminary bookings and reservations on equipment you need to hire very early on in the pre-production period. While it may not always be possible to do so, for obvious reasons you should try to avoid making firm commitments to spend money before the foregoing steps have been completed. Once you have completed your budget preparations (and script breakdown where appropriate) you are in a position to go ahead and make commitments in terms of securing the crew and equipment you need.

Equipment needs to be booked as soon as possible, consistent with the advice given in the paragraph above. This means that not only will you be well placed to secure the items you require, but you will have time to negotiate deals or packages at advantageous rates, always well worth the effort.

Crewing should similarly be undertaken as soon as practicable so that you can provide the project with the appropriate mix of technical and creative talent for the kind of programme you are producing. Production Managers have invaluable experience of the strengths and foibles of directors, sound recordists and other members of the team and can play an important role in constructing the right crew for the task ahead.

The recce and location finding are among the most important tasks to be undertaken in pre-production (see Chapter 5) and while the Production

Manager may not be directly involved, nevertheless will need to be fully informed of developments here as the selection of locations has an important impact on budgets, not just in the direct cost or facility fee but in many other areas too, such as transport and travel, as well as travelling time and insurance. Information from the recce needs to be fed back to production management as soon as possible so that relevant information can be added to schedules, contact lists and call sheets.

Risk assessments will be carried out at this stage for all elements of the proposed shoot (Chapter 7). It is usually the responsibility of the production management team to ensure that every member of the crew has the appropriate Health and Safety training for the work they are to undertake in the situation in which it is to be undertaken. It may, for instance, be necessary to book a director or cameraman onto a hazardous situations course so that they are properly prepared for working in dangerous situations. Remember too that although someone may indeed have completed such a course, a refresher session may be recommended or even mandatory. Last minute crew changes can be particularly difficult in such circumstances and it is important not to overlook these matters should such a situation arise.

Schedules, call sheets and contact sheets will be prepared as information becomes available, placing great demands on the time, patience and ingenuity of those responsible for production management. Systems need to be in place so that vital pieces of information are logged onto forms and not lost on scraps of paper which are apt to disappear. More detailed information on these items is to be found in Chapter 5 along with suggestions for appropriate basic form design.

Licences/clearances may well be more appropriately dealt with in production and post-production but it is worth also considering negotiations in pre-production, especially if the material involved is central to the production. If permission to use the material is not forthcoming, or not forthcoming at an acceptable licensing fee, then it is well to be aware of this as soon as possible so that some workaround or alternative can be sought. Clients or commissioners will not be impressed if material has to be removed from the programme in post-production because negotiations have not been successful. You should also consider ensuring that your clearance paperwork is up to date and that release forms are available for the use of location crews before shooting begins.

Shot logging will obviously not take place until production begins. The task is included in the pre-production check-list so that the appropriate logging forms can be prepared and made available before they are needed. A sample logging form is provided on the web site associated with this book.

9
Production

Production check-list
Risk assessment*
Insurance arrangements
Security
Contact sheets*
Call sheets*
Purchase orders*
Equipment
Check equipment
Arrange catering/subsistence
Arrange travel and transport
Arrange accommodation
Production publicity/stills, etc.
Release forms*
* Indicates that an associated form is available on-line

Figure 9.1 Production check-list

The fact that our production check-list is considerably shorter than that for pre-production underlines the importance of timely and thorough pre-production preparation. This should ensure that those responsible for production management will be better able to cope with the inevitable crises and changes of plan which are to be expected in any production.

Risk assessment, it might be argued, has already featured in the check-list for pre-production. It appears again here as a timely and important reminder that Health and Safety is an ongoing concern (Chapter 7) and needs to be constantly reassessed. Remember too that the recommended fifth step in risk assessment is to *Review and Revise*. Production Managers should consider it one of their most important functions to remind all members of the production team to revisit their risk assessments and to revise and update where necessary.

Insurance arrangements should already have been made before shooting begins, but again it is worth double-checking that all eventualities have been considered, that cover is indeed in place and takes account of any material changes in the timing and content of the production since the original cover was secured.

Security is an important issue not otherwise dealt with in this book. There are many situations during production and shooting where security needs to be carefully considered. I am thinking here of security as distinct from the safety aspects as dealt with in Chapter 7. Production Managers need to be satisfied that proper arrangements have been made to take reasonable precautions against the loss of equipment, vehicles and personal belongings in all circumstances. There are situations, however, which raise particular problems such as remote locations, inner city areas and night shoots where special arrangements might have to be made and the services of professional security companies engaged. There are no hard and fast rules except that security needs to be carefully considered and sensible precautions taken. Under no circumstances should equipment be left unattended in vehicles overnight, however tempting it might be to do so. Saving ten minutes at the end of the day might easily result in the delay of a day or more if vital gear goes missing before morning!

Contact sheets and call sheets which will, of course, have been prepared during pre-production need to be kept under review and updated where circumstances have been changed and where there have been changes in personnel. In particular those responsible for production management will require to ensure that details of emergency contact numbers are easily accessible from as many of the production documents as possible. There is no real harm in duplicating this information in various places so that it comes easily to hand. Emergency contacts should not consist simply of the home number of the executive producer and the Production Manager! Local and accurate information about contacts for police and other services is essential on location. A crew should not need to call the production office for such information when there is no guarantee that the person who has access to the information will be at their desk when help is needed. You may for instance have had to liaise in advance with traffic police about some of the shooting you are undertaking, in which case relevant numbers and names need to be available in case changes need to be made to these arrangements at the last minute.

Purchase orders should have been set up and be in regular use but it is worthwhile ensuring during production stages that all members of the team are complying with the system you have put in place, otherwise the ongoing monitoring of your budget (see below) will not be as accurate as you need it to be.

Budget reports enable the proper financial management of your production. More detail is provided in Chapter 4 and a simple spreadsheet to help you to do this is included on this book's web site. Maintaining the budgets and producing reports is one of the vital aspects of the work of production management. The ability to capture an instant snapshot of the state of the budget will be of enormous help, not only in reassuring you that you are within budget, but in making rational and well-informed decisions when extra expenditure is requested.

Equipment which has been ordered needs to be delivered or collected and it is often the job of the Production Manager to ensure that this takes place as and when specified. Although it should not be necessary, it is as well for you to consider it as part of your job to remind those who are about to use any equipment to check that it is working before setting out on location. Check-lists of equipment might well also be invaluable not only in assisting the crew to double check that they have what they need and to check that it is working, but also to ensure that equipment taken on location is returned and not left hidden and neglected in some shady spot on location. Needless to say, batteries need to be recharged and this task should perhaps be specified on your equipment check-list.

Catering, accommodation, travel and transport will often but not always have been dealt with at pre-production. It is not always possible to specify such arrangements in advance, though it is to be recommended that you do so as early as possible. Booking ahead can also bring budgetary benefits. Inevitably, however, it is likely that PMs will have to make arrangements during a production, and this item on the check-list is a reminder that it is no bad thing to check that arrangements already made do still meet the requirements of a production schedule which might have changed.

Release forms are possibly of greater relevance to factual and documentary productions than to other genres, which will probably have already issued contracts to artists and extras. Forms should have been prepared in pre-production, but it should be made clear who precisely is to be responsible for the completion of these forms on location. This is particularly important as this is hardly one of the most popular tasks in a production and will be avoided by most of the team if at all possible. The work should be entrusted to someone (usually a production assistant if you have one) who can be relied upon not only to obtain the necessary signatures but to return the documents safely to the production office.

Publicity and stills may or may not be the responsibility of production management. Drama and feature productions are less likely to forget this aspect of their responsibilities; indeed they may even have access to a unit publicist. Other less well-funded projects may have to undertake this work themselves. Documentary and factual programme-makers are less likely to build such considerations into the production period. This is a pity and publicity is certainly worth considering as part of your regular check-list of useful things to initiate and keep track of during the shoot, even if it only comprises of ensuring that someone takes photographs.

10
Post-production

Post-production check-list		
Risk assessment*		
Book editing		
Book dubbing		
Special effects		
Graphics		
Licenses*		
Shot/tape logging*		
Music logging*		
Music clearances*		
Compliance checks		
Compile paperwork		
* indicates that an associated form is available on-line		

Figure 10.1 Post-production check-list

Risk assessment appears on our check-list for the third time. This usefully underlines the importance of the issue but is not the principal reason that it appears in post-production, when all the shooting has been completed. This entry is intended as a reminder that risk assessment forms need to be collected and compiled with other paperwork (see below). In order to do so, it may well be necessary to remind other members of the team to complete their forms and to sign them off. When and if they fail to do so, you will need to chase them.

Logging is an essential prerequisite for the edit. This will usually be carried out by the director or another member of the production team. Ensuring that all shots are logged, together with minimal remarks on the quality and suitability of the take will make editing simpler and more efficient. A simple form will suffice for factual programmes. Drama productions require a slightly more sophisticated approach and the ability to make a record which includes scene and take information. Whatever the genre, shot logging is vital; nothing is more frustrating and wasteful of resources than hunting for an elusive shot while the edit suite (and possibly the editor) is idle.

Editing and dubbing take place in post-production. If these tasks are to be carried out in-house, equipment will have to be reserved and if necessary a freelance editor engaged to work on the project. In many cases editing will happen in an outside facility and if a sound dub is required this is more than likely to require the expertise of a specialist company. In both these cases therefore, the Production Manager will be responsible for booking the facilities well enough in advance and where possible to negotiate a block booking rate for the production.

Special effects and graphics may be commissioned as early as possible in post-production. With the only proviso being that they are ready in good time for the edit, it is probably not a good idea to commission too early so that there is time for changes to be made to the final content of the programme. It might be a good idea to design your own form for the content of graphics and credits. This can provide a useful check on the accuracy of information and spelling and provides a way of *signing off* the accuracy of on-screen information.

Music logging wherever possible should take place at the time and place the music is used, normally in the edit suite. The risk of vital information and even original discs being mislaid will be minimised if this practice is observed. Every occurrence of a passage of music requires to be separately logged, and as much information as possible entered on the relevant paperwork. Hours can be wasted trying to trace that short piece of music whose details have disappeared; good practice in the edit suite will avoid such an eventuality.

Music clearances for any sources other than library music need to be carefully negotiated well in advance of use, and relevant paperwork kept on file for future reference.

Licences for any third-party material used in post-production are essential. Broadcasters will reject programmes where there is not a clear agreement for the use of material from archives or other sources. The use of material which is not cleared and licensed leaves the production company open to litigation.

Compliance checks (Chapter 7) will ensure that the production has complied with relevant laws and regulations and if necessary the commissioner's compliance officer will have been consulted and all correspondence retained.

Compiling the paperwork is the final task of production management and will ensure that all the papers, forms and correspondence relating to a programme are kept in a form which is both coherent and accessible. Future exploitation of a programme could be inhibited if licences and clearances cannot be traced. A good filing system is essential. Production Managers move from programme to programme, and if they are freelance, from employer to employer. A critical measure of their effectiveness is the degree to which a successor can locate the programme file, find the information and make sense of it.

Directory of agencies and organisations

BBC Training & Development
35 Marylebone High Street
London W1U 4PX
t: 0870 122 0216
w: www.bbctraining.com
e: training@bbc.co.uk

British Academy of Composers and Songwriters
26 Berners Street
London W1T 3LR
t: 0207 636 2929
f: 0207 636 2212
w: www.britishacademy.com

Celtx
PO Box 23126
St John's, NL A1B 4J9
Canada
w: www.celtx.com
e: info@celtx.com

Documentary Filmmakers Group
4th Floor, Shacklewell Studios
28 Shacklewell Lane
London E8 2EZ
t: 020 7249 6600
w: www.dfgdocs.com
e: info@dfgdocs.com
(Good for sample forms, etc. specifically aimed at factual programme-makers)

Equity
Guild House
Upper St Martin's Lane,
London WC2H 9EG
t: 020 7379 6000
f: 020 7379 7001
w: www.equity.org.uk
e: info@equity.org.uk

Guild of International Songwriters and Composers
Sovereign House
12 Trewartha Road
Praa Sands, Penzance
Cornwall TR20 9ST
t: 01736 762826
f: 01736 763328
w: www.songwriters-guild.co.uk
e: songmag@aol.com

Health and Safety Executive (HSE)
t: Infoline: 0845 345 0055
w: www.hse.gov.uk

Indie Training Fund
3rd Floor,
18–20 Southwark Street
London SE1 1TJ
t: 020 7407 0454
w: www.pact.co.uk/training/itf/

MCPS-PRS Alliance
Copyright House
29–33 Berners St
London W1T 3AB
t: 020 7580 5544
w: www.mcps-prs-alliance.co.uk

Musicians' Union
33 Palfrey Place
London SW8 1PE
t: 020 7840 5504
f: 020 7840 5599
e: london@musiciansunion.org.uk
(See also various national/regional offices)

National Film and Television School
Beaconsfield Studios
Station Road
Beaconsfield
Bucks HP9 1LG
t: 01494 671234
w: www.nftsfilm-tv.ac.uk

Ofcom (Office of Communications)
Riverside House
2a Southwark Bridge Road
London SE1 9HA
t: 020 7981 3000
w: www.ofcom.org.uk

Open Office (Open source office software suite)
w: www.openoffice.org

PACT
Procter House
1 Procter Street
Holborn
London WC1V 6DW
t: 020 7067 4367
w: www.pact.co.uk

Production Managers Association
Ealing Studios
Ealing Green
Ealing
London W5 5EP
t: 020 8758 8699
w: www.pma.org.uk
e: pma@pma.org.uk

Skillset
Focus Point
21 Caledonian Road
London N1 9GB
t: 020 7713 98000
w: www.skillset.org
e: info@skillset.org

Skillset Scotland
249 West George Street
Glasgow G2 4QE
t: 0141 222 2633

Skillset Northern Ireland
Scottish Mutual Building
Room 24, 16 Donegall Square South
Belfast BT1 5JA
t: 02890 434 075

Skillset Cymru
33–35 West Bute Street
Cardiff CF10 5LH
t: 029 2045 2832

Writers' Guild of Great Britain
15 Britannia Street
London WC1X 9JN
t: 020 7833 0777
f: 020 7833 4777
w: www.writersguild.org.uk

Glossary

Above-the-line: Costs incurred before the start of the project.

Assignment: The transfer of (in this context) intellectual property to another party.

Below-the-line: Costs incurred in production and post-production.

Blood chit: See **release form** (below). The origins of the term are obscure but appear to have military origins.

Breakdown or script breakdown: The process of analysing a script and 'breaking it down' into its constituent parts.

Call-sheet: A document outlining the times various members of the production team are required on location or on set.

Clearance(s): A (signed) agreement consenting to the use of specified material, for example, a clip or an interview within an audiovisual production.

Competent person: A person with the relevant skills, training and experience to undertake a particular task.

Compliance: A rather general term which refers to the need to observe the many laws, regulations and agreements which govern television production.

Cash flow: The movement of cash in and out of your business or production.

Collecting Society: An independent organisation which collects fees on behalf of its members. Composers, musicians and music copyright holders are often members of collecting societies, such as MCPS-PRS Alliance.

Contact-sheet: A document containing relevant contact information for each member of the crew and cast so they can be contacted as and when required.

Contingency: A small percentage of the total budget set aside to cover unforeseen expense.

Cost centre: A heading which allows expenditure of certain types to be grouped together.

Department: A distinctive discipline or expertise within a production, for example, set building, wardrobe.

Equity rate: The (minimum) rate of pay for a particular job undertaken by an artist negotiated by the trade union Equity with a number of organisations, for example, PACT, C4.

H&S: Health and Safety.

Indie: Industry shorthand for Independent Production Company, as distinct from a broadcasting organisation such as the BBC or ITV.

Licence: An agreement whereby a copyright holder agrees to the use of its material under specified conditions and usually for a specified term.

Notional: A figure or sum in the budget which is based more on experience and refined 'guess-work' than on a particular scale of charges.

OB: Outside Broadcast.

OFCOM: Office of Communications.

PM: Industry shorthand for the Production Manager.

PA: In the media industries usually production assistant, though it can refer to the more generic 'personal assistant'.

PACT: Producers' Alliance for Cinema & Television

Post: Often used to shorten the term 'post-production'.

Production board: A physical, wall-mounted board holding coloured strips of paper corresponding to each scene in a feature and containing information relevant to it.

Production Coordinator: A responsible but junior production management role often involved in booking equipment and facilities, book-keeping, etc. A possible career step before becoming a Production Manager.

Production management: The diligent oversight and direction of all the processes and procedures which are required in order to safely and legally accomplish a finished programme on time and on budget.

Production strip: See production board above; the actual, physical strip of paper containing information about that scene.

Recce: Literally to reconnoitre in order to assess the suitability of and gain information about proposed locations, etc.

Release (or release form): The form of agreement between producer and participant outlining the terms and conditions of use. Sometimes referred to as a *blood chit*.

Risk assessment: A careful and documented consideration of what could cause harm to people.

Schedule: A list containing information about times and locations for shooting specific sections of the programme.

Further reading

Few books are available which deal directly with production management for television, especially in the UK context.

Production Management for Film and Video Gates, Richard (2003) Focal Press does so, but is stronger in the film context and is less helpful in terms of television production.

Other titles include:

Film Production Management Cleve, Bastian (2006) Focal Press is written from an American perspective as are most books dealing with this subject.

Surviving Production Patz, Deborah (1997) Michael Wiese Productions is by an American author.

Index

CPSIA information can be obtained
at www.ICGtesting.com
Printed in the USA
LVOW01s0006211216
518216LV00007B/126/P